DR. SEBI HERPES

DR. SEBI'S METHOD TO GET RID FOREVER OF COLD SORES AND GENITAL HERPES

Table of Contents

INTRODUCTION...3

CHAPTER 1: HERPES SIMPLEX VIRUS 6

CHAPTER 2: GENITAL HERPES 8

CHAPTER 3: HERPES PLUS CAUSES..20

CHAPTER 4: HERPES DIAGNOSIS TESTING..21

CHAPTER 5: SIGNS AND SYMPTOMS OF HERPES..22

CHAPTER 6: THE HERPES VIRUS HEALING METHOD & DR. SEBI...................25

CHAPTER 7: FAQS ABOUT DR. SEBI CURE FOR HERPES 40

CHAPTER 8: WHY IS DR SEBI TREATMENT SUCCESSFUL 42

CHAPTER 9: ALKALINE RECIPES FOR HERPES CURE 45

CONCLUSION 58

Introduction

Dr. Sebi is a physician, botanist, organic chemist, and naturalist. He has studied herbs in North, Central and South America, Africa and the Caribbean, and has developed a new methodology and system related to the repair of the human body with herbs that have established themselves as real estate in more than 30 years of experience.

On November 26, 1933 Dr. Sebi was born Alfredo Bowman in Ilanga, Honduras, Spain. Dr. Sebi is a self-taught man. His adorable grandmother, "Mama Hay," encouraged him to respect life's experiences. The beginning of the game and her perception of the stream and the forested area, combined with her grandmother's guidance, helped Sebi establish himself to be submissive to the Truth in his future life.

Dr Sebi went to the United States as a self-taught man who was determined to suffer from asthma, diabetes, impotence, and dementia. After unsuccessful drugs with ordinary specialists and conventional western drugs, Sebi was a guide for a botanist in Mexico. Discovering amazingly repetitive accomplishments of all his problems, he began to make regular blends of plant-based nutritional cells between cell cleansing and rejuvenation of the significant number of cells that make up the human body.

Sebi did dedicate over 30 years of his life to creating an interesting technique that could go through long periods of observational information. creating an interesting technique that could go through long periods of observational information.

Motivated by the personal experience and information he received, he began to transmit the mixtures to other people who brought Dr. Sebi Cell Food.

Alfredo Bowman, otherwise called Dr. Sebi, was a self-declared healer and cultivator. He was self-taught — he was not a clinical specialist and held no Ph.D.

A eulogy depicts his questionable wellbeing claims, for example, relieving AIDS and leukemia. These and comparable declarations brought about a 1993 claim that finished with the court requesting Dr. Sebi's association to quit making these cases. Dr. Sebi apparently kicked the bucket in 2016 in police guardianship.

Dr. Sebi accepted the Western way to deal with malady to be incapable. He held that bodily fluid and acridity — rather microscopic organisms and infections, for instance — caused malady.

A fundamental hypothesis behind the diet is that malady can just make due in acidic situations. The point of the diet is to accomplish an alkaline state in the body so as to prevent or destroy illness.

The diet's authentic site sells natural cures that it cases will detoxify the body.

The site connects to no exploration that would bolster its cases about medical advantages. It notes that the Food and Drug Administration (FDA) have not assessed the announcements. Those behind the site recognize that they are not clinical specialists and don't expect the site's substance to supplant clinical counsel.

As indicated by Dr. Sebi, malady is an aftereffect of bodily fluid developing in an area of your body. For instance, the development of bodily fluid in the lungs is pneumonia, while abundance bodily fluid in the pancreas is diabetes. He contends that ailments can't exist in an alkaline domain and start to happen when your body turns out to be excessively acidic. By carefully following his diet and utilizing his restrictive expensive supplements, he vows to reestablish your body's common basic state and detoxify your unhealthy body.

Initially, Dr. Sebi guaranteed that this diet could fix conditions like AIDS, sickle cell pallor, leukemia, and lupus. So, after a 1993 claim, he was requested to end making such claims. The diet comprises of a particular rundown of affirmed vegetables, organic products, grains, nuts, seeds, oils, and herbs. As animal are not allowed, the Dr. Sebi diet is viewed as a vegetarian diet. Sebi asserted that for your body to recuperate itself, you should follow the diet reliably for amazing results.

At last, while numerous individuals declared that the program has fixed them, no logical examinations supported these cases. Advocates guarantee that it diminishes the risk of sickness when combined with explicit supplements sold on the diet's site.

Dr. Sebi admitted that human fluid and acridity caused sickness. He held that consuming certain foods and sustaining an imperative distance from others could detoxify the body, accomplishing an alkaline express that could diminish the hazard and impacts of diseases.

The Dr. Sebi diet isn't validated by authentic sources, and no relevant evidence shows that it can prevent or treat illnesses. Plant-based diets can improve wellbeing beneath certain situations, yet the Dr. Sebi diet may suspend enough key supplements to keep the body healthy.

A Honduran man with humble beginnings, Dr. Sebi made extraordinary walks in the realm of common wellbeing and health with the making of his particular diet that includes things like seeded natural products (stay away from seedless organic products), olive oil, agave syrup, coconut oil, wild rice and that's only the tip of the iceberg.

Dr. Sebi accepted that there were six principal nutrition types: live, raw, dead, half breed, hereditarily altered, and tranquilizes.

His diet basically cut out all the nutritional categories with the exception of live and raw, urging weight watchers to eat as near a raw vegetarian diet as could be possible under the circumstances. This includes foods like normally developed leafy foods, just as whole grains.

Dr. Sebi accepted that the raw and live foods were "electric," which battled the acidic food waste in the body. With his diet, Dr. Sebi created a list of foods that he viewed as the best for his diet and named this the Dr. Sebi Electric Food List. Significantly after his passing, his list keeps on developing and improving.

Adhering to the Dr Sebi Diet and Dr Sebi Food List can be troublesome if you eat out a great deal. Subsequently, you ought to become accustomed to creating a lot of vegetarian diet dinners at home (utilizing agave syrup, olive oil, wild rice, and so forth).

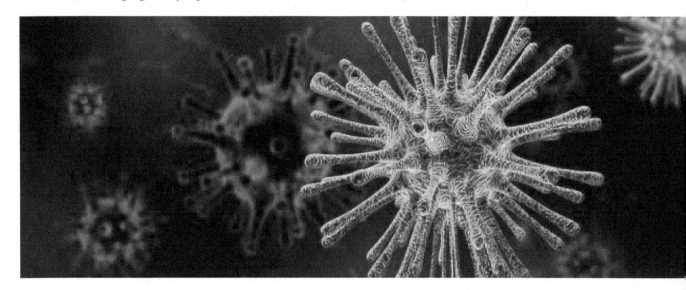

Chapter 1: Herpes Simplex Virus

Herpes is a latent, dormant virus that can enter the body through simple skin-to-skin contact, which is because the opportunistic bug can take advantage of even microscopic points of entry. Condoms can prevent infection, but not always. In truth, unless you become a celibate monk and move to a monastery by yourself, you'll never be 100% safe.

Two kinds of herpes simplex virus: HSV-1 and HSV-2. Both viruses have different forms of behavior. HSV-1 embeds itself (usually) in the trigeminal ganglion (facial nerve cells), while HSV-2 prefers the sacral ganglion—going after your private parts (genital herpes).

The virus is extremely handy and has been reported in various parts of the body. Although these are its preferred areas to inhabit, it's certainly possible to acquire HSV-1 in your genitals and HSV-2 on your face. However, such incidences are uncommon.

The virus "stashes" itself into these nerve cells. When the conditions are right, it starts to replicate itself again, attacking your healthy cells and traveling upward, emerging as a red pimple-like sore before your body fights it off. Sometimes, when the virus "wakes up," you'll experience mild flu-like symptoms, including a fever and sore throat, which is why cold sores are called "cold" sores.

Besides, herpes typically creates onset symptoms upon initial infection. So, if you contract herpes the first time, you'll not only come down with a herpes sore (on your genitals or your mouth), but you'll also feel sick for several days.

However, it does not always occur, and as with many things herpes-related, it seems to be primarily dependent on your bodies' immune system.

Overall, herpes is one of nature's most "successful" viruses. It exists in our bodies forever, is extremely easy to contract, and it (typically) does not harm or kill the host.

Reminders you should know:

- Herpes can be transmitted sexually even when there are no blisters on the skin.

- HSV-2 can be transmitted whether you're wearing a condom or not.

- When you contract HSV-1, your antibodies will prevent you from contracting the virus a second time in another part of your body.

- However, the presence of HSV-1 will not protect you from HSV-2, which is why many people have both at the same time.

- Herpes zoster or "shingles" is related to varicella or chickenpox virus. This virus behaves similarly to herpes simplex by embedding itself and reemerging in the form of blisters later in life. Chickenpox itself is considered a type of herpes infection.

- It's estimated that 70% of the U.S. population is infected with HSV-1 and around 30% with HSV-2.

Chapter 2: Genital Herpes

Genital herpes is a herpes simplex virus (HSV) viral infection that causes painful blisters on the genitals and surrounding areas.

This virus has two forms: types 1 and 2: HSV-1 and HSV-2.

Genital herpes, especially in people aged 20 to 24, is a common condition.

Sites where the herpes virus is affected:

- Genitalia

  - The anus and perianal region

- Buttocks

- The upper half of the glute

- Mouth

- Lips or ears •

- Facial herpes, which involves cold sores, results from inflammation on the lips or ears.

Infections By The Herpes Virus

The virus, either through a lesion on the skin or through the lining of the mouth and genital region, invades the human body.

The virus uses material from the host cell to replicate until it is within the human cell (a replication process).

The cell is killed in this process. The characteristic signs (blisters, etc.) and symptoms (tingling, pain, etc.) of a herpetic episode are responsible for killing the host cell.

Virus particles infiltrate sensory nerve fibers at the infection site and continue to migrate to where the fiber starts, in addition to entering and taking control of cells at the injection site.

Fibers of the sensory nerve carry signals that allow us to feel pain, touch, cold, light, etc. From a small cluster of cells known as the sensory ganglion, sensory nerve fibers start.

The virus settles at the base of the skull in a ganglion, known as the trigeminal ganglion, in the case of facial herpes. The virus takes shelter in genital herpes in the sacral ganglion, found at the end of the spinal cord.

When the virus enters the lymph node, it stays there for the remainder of our lives. In the ganglion, HSV is reactivated regularly, and virus particles migrate to the skin or mucosa through the nerve fiber, causing repeated symptoms.

Not the only infection many of us deal with is herpes simplex. The varicella-zoster virus hosts someone who has had chickenpox. While it can reactivate, this virus remains largely dormant, but only very rarely.

The virus particles leave the nerve ganglia when this occurs, migrate down the nerve fibers to the skin, and cause herpetic lesions.

Once a virus enters our body, to combat it, antibodies are made. Antibodies are present in the blood and are necessary for the natural protection of the body (immune response).

After the initial episode, they continue to be produced for several weeks. The antibodies help make chronic symptoms milder than the first episode in the case of genital herpes.

It is important to note that the detection of antibodies in the blood of people who have never undergone a genital herpes episode is very normal.

The episode was either so mild that the person did not know that it was occurring, or that it was diagnosed as another illness, or that there were no signs at all, and so it was not known as such.

Infection of genital herpes occurs by interaction of the genitals with the virus present in an active herpes partner (this can result from genital or oral contact).

Primary or initial infection is called the first episode, and it is at this point, certain viruses are housed in the nerve ganglia.

When the virus replicates in the ganglion, subsequent episodes, known as recurrences, occur, releasing virus particles that migrate down the nerve back to the original infection site. ·

Infection Sites for Genital Herpes

In women, the vulva and the entrance to the vagina are the most frequently affected genital regions. Lesions may also develop on the cervix occasionally.

Lesions on the gland (end of the penis), foreskin, and shaft of the penis are most common in males. Sores on the testicles can grow sometimes.

Less commonly, injuries around the anus, buttocks, and upper thigh can occur in both men and women.

Recurrent Herpes Virus Infections

Some people do not experience recurrences with symptoms, but they are generally shorter and less severe than those who do the initial episode.

Over time, recurrences can decrease in both severity and frequency, although there is no definitive evidence that this happens.

Recurrences are usually preceded by warning symptoms such as tingling, itching, burning, or pain.

As with the initial episode, there is great variation in people's experiences of recurrence.

About 80% of those with a first episode caused by HSV-2 will have at least one recurrence, while only 50% of people with HSV-1 will experience a recurrence.

The frequency of recurrence is four to five times in the first two years after being infected.

Genital Herpes Can Be Escapable

Since there are sometimes little to no initial signs, at least eight out of 10 people who bear the virus do not know they have been infected.

However, the virus may be triggered by such stimuli, triggering an outbreak of genital herpes.

The severity of the symptoms of genital herpes can differ greatly from person to person.

The initial episode may be so mild as to go unnoticed, and several years after the first outbreak, a first recurrence can occur.

Up to 60% of individuals with genital HSV infection show no symptoms and do not know they are infected with the disease. However, these individuals are capable of transmitting the virus to others.

In such cases, in individuals unable to understand the sudden onset of the infection and the apparent transmission from another individual, a genital herpes occurrence may lead to confusion and bewilderment.

What Triggers Genital Herpes?

The initial episode usually occurs 2 to 12 days after sexual contact with a person with an active infection.

Recurrence occurs when the virus replicates in the nerve ganglia. The virus particles travel down the nerve to the site of primary infection on the skin or mucous membranes (e.g., the moist epithelium of the mouth, vagina, etc.).

Although it is unknown exactly why the virus reactivates several times, the causal factors can be separated between physical and psychological.

Physical

Physical factors differ from person to person:

- Be exhausted

- Suffering from other genital infections (affecting the local skin area)

- The menstruation

- Drink lots of alcohol

- Exposure of the area to strong sunlight

- Conditions that make a person immunocompromised (when the immune system is not working normally)

- Prolonged periods of stress

Friction or damage to the skin, caused, for example, by sexual intercourse, can also lead to a recurrence.

In short, anything that lowers your immune system or causes local damage can trigger recurrences.

Psychological

Recent research indicates that more frequent recurrences can be triggered by periods of prolonged stress. As a consequence of experiencing repetitions, it is often normal to feel tension and anxiety.

Transmission of infection

People with herpes can infect when symptoms of a herpes episode occur and no symptoms.

People who experience an episode of herpes, be it facial or genital, should be considered infectious from the beginning of the episode until the last ulcer has healed.

Facial herpes lesions (e.g., cold sores) are also a source of transmission with the practice of oral sex. Consequently, oral sex should be avoided if a partner has a facial herpes attack.

The infectious virus may still be present in people without obvious lesions during periods of asymptomatic virus shedding. This asymptomatic spread cannot be predicted but is known to occur at least 5% of days.

Occasionally, a partner in a long-term relationship may develop herpes symptoms for the first time. Often this is because one or both partners are carriers of HSV without knowing it.

The chance to transmit herpes can be reduced by avoiding sex when signs of herpes are present and condoms in the periods between episodes.

What Does It Mean To Have Genital Herpes?

Primary genital HSV infection can be severe and involve generalized flu-like symptoms.

This can lead to dejection, combined with the pain and discomfort of injuries and, in some instances, a secondary bacterial infection.

Fortunately, recovery is quick once the blisters have healed.

Sexual Relations

People with recurrent genital herpes may rethink some aspects of sexual intimacy. They use non-genital forms of sexual interaction during an active episode, for example.

This also means considering whether, how, and when you will tell your sexual partner that you have genital herpes.

Given the social stigma that seems to surround genital herpes, it's best to prepare your thoughts in advance before telling someone.

Most people respond by being supportive when you confess, and they appreciate and respect your courage and honesty. This person chooses not to tell their sexual partner risks carrying fear, guilt, and secrecy.

In developing a relationship where both parties fully understand the possibility of transmission, the decision not to use a condom can be agreed upon.

For people who experience frequent herpes recurrences and whose sexual intercourse pattern is severely disturbed, antiviral therapy reduces recurrences' frequency. It can help regain a more acceptable sex life.

Fertility

Genital herpes is not hereditary. The virus does not affect fertility and is not transmitted through a woman's sperm or eggs.

Treatment

While there is no remedy for genital herpes, antiviral drugs can normally regulate symptoms.

Inconvenience

Blisters caused by the herpes virus may become infected by bacteria in rare cases. It may cause a skin infection that can spread to other areas of the body, such as your lips, hands, or fingers if this occurs.

The virus may spread to other parts of the body in rare cases, such as the brain, eyes, liver, or lungs.

People with a compromised immune system, such as people with HIV or others who use certain drugs, are at greater risk for these complications.

Herpes Neonatal

Neonatal herpes happens at the time of birth when a baby becomes infected with the herpes virus. It can be extreme and, in some circumstances, fatal. It is a rare disorder, however.

Treatment Of Genital Herpes

Oral antiviral medications can partially control the signs and symptoms of genital herpes when used to treat primary infection and recurrent infections or when used as daily suppressive therapy for 12 months or longer.

However, these drugs do not clear the virus from the body or affect the risk, frequency, or severity of recurrences after stopping the drug.

Antiviral treatment applied to the skin in the form of a cream or ointment is not recommended since the benefits derived from its application are minimal.

Treatment Of Primary Infection

If you have genital herpes for the first time, you will need to be treated with an antiviral medicine for 7 to 10 days. Acyclovir, famciclovir, or valacyclovir are used.

These drugs work by preventing the virus from multiplying. However, they do not clear the virus from your body completely.

Treatment Of Recurrent Outbreaks

In case of mild symptoms

If symptoms are mild, your doctor may suggest treatment to relieve your symptoms without the need for medication:

- Keep the affected area clean using water or salt. This will help prevent infection of the blisters or ulcers and help them heal faster. It will also prevent the affected areas from sticking together.

- Apply an ice pack wrapped in a towel or cool, wet tea bags on the ulcers to help soothe pain and speed up the healing process.

- Do not apply ice directly to the skin.

- Apply petroleum jelly, or numbing cream, such as 5% lidocaine, to the blisters or ulcers to reduce pain when urinating.

- Drink plenty of fluids to dilute your urine. This will make it less painful when passing urine. Urinating while sitting in a bathroom or while pouring water over your genitals can also help.

- Avoid wearing tight clothing, as it can irritate blisters and ulcers.

In case of severe symptoms

If your symptoms are more severe, an antiviral medication may be prescribed. You can use acyclovir, famciclovir, or valaciclovir, which you will have to take five times a day for five days.

Episodic And Suppressive Antiviral Therapy

Episodic therapy

Suppose you have fewer than six recurring outbreaks of genital herpes in a year. In that case, your doctor may prescribe a five-day course of acyclovir each time you experience tingling or numbness before symptoms begin. This is known as episodic treatment.

Episodic therapy is most effective when taken as soon as possible after the onset of symptoms, usually tingling and pain in the affected skin.

Episodic therapy helps relieve symptoms and shortens each acute episode's duration but does not affect attacks' frequency.

Suppressive therapy

If you have more than six outbreaks of genital herpes that recur in a year, or if your symptoms are particularly severe and causing a lot of discomforts, you may need to take an antiviral medicine every day as part of a long-term treatment plan.

Suppressive therapy involves taking antiviral medication every day for long periods (usually 12 months). The patient, together with the doctor, decides to suspend treatment or continue for longer periods.

Suppressive therapy stops the multiplication of the virus, and treatment can:

• Reduce the number of acute pictures of genital herpes, or prevent them completely.

• Reduce the frequency of virus transmission without showing symptoms.

Find that your pictures' frequency is very high, or you find it difficult emotionally to cope with the fact of suffering from genital herpes. You can discuss this with your doctor and discuss the use of suppressive therapy with him.

Is Suppressive Therapy Appropriate For Me?

The use of suppressive therapy can vary, and it is important to speak with your doctor about whether this option is appropriate for you. Your doctor may agree that suppressive therapy is appropriate if you:

• It presents a frequency of its recurrences that, in its opinion, is unacceptably high.

• Suffers from particularly severe and long-lasting high-frequency frames

• Find that recurrences of genital herpes make you depressed, anxious or withdrawn, or the emotional disturbance is hurting your social activities and sex life. These feelings can themselves cause a recurrence, resulting in a vicious cycle. Suppressive therapy, perhaps only for a few months, can help you break the cycle and give you a sense of control over the infection.

- You experience severe pain (neuralgia) during recurring episodes.

- You have pictures that tend to occur during specific situations, for example, when you have exams or go on vacation, or you do not want to spoil a special event such as a honeymoon with a recurrence. Suppressive therapy in these situations should minimize the chances of a recurrence.

- You've got recurrences when you start a new relationship. In this case, suppressive therapy can give you more confidence.

- You know that stress is a trigger for your recurrences, and you are going through a stressful period (e.g., a new job or the recent death of a family member).

- You have another illness that triggers a recurrence of herpes (a series of suppressive therapy may be appropriate until the other condition has resolved).

How long will I need to take the treatment?

Usually, 12 months. If, after this period, you still have problems with recurrent infections, then you can, together with your doctor, decide whether to continue suppressive therapy.

Will suppressive therapy make a living with genital herpes easier?

Many people find that being able to control their herpes boosts their sense of well-being and self-confidence. Even if taken for a few months, suppressive therapy can help end the depression and anxiety caused by recurrent genital herpes.

If you find your condition difficult to cope with, you must seek expert support from your doctor or counselor. You can also join a patient support group in your area.

Many people who contact a support group find it helpful. Also, close friends or your partner can continue to be an important support source and help you overcome anxiety or depression caused by genital herpes.

Will suppressive therapy prevent me from spreading my infection?

Although we know that suppressive therapy reduces the chance that the virus will spread during and between recurrences, it is not known whether it protects your sexual partners from contracting herpes virus infection.

Condoms are not proven to protect against transmission of genital herpes, but they are considered helpful and should be used.

You are primarily at risk of transmitting the infection when you have symptoms of genital herpes. It is at these times when it is most advisable to avoid sexual contact.

Chapter 3: Herpes Plus Causes

There are some primary causes of herpes, which I am going to talk about below:

Oral Sex

Oral sex is good, and I do not deny it, but it is wise for us to know who and how healthy our partner's mouth is. If the mouth of the person giving you a leader has cold sores around his/her mouth, there is a tendency that you might get infected with herpes.

Unprotected Sex

Having unprotected sex with someone suffering from herpes transmits the virus.

Sharing sex toys with someone infected with the herpes virus transmits the virus rapidly and very fast.

Transmitted Through Birth

Another craziest thing about this virus is that it can be transmitted from the mother to her newborn baby through birth delivery if the mother's genital herpes have sores while giving birth.

Please note that the sharing of towels, chairs, kitchen utensils, or toilet seats with someone with herpes cannot get you infected because the viruses need a moist environment to be transmitted. That is why it can be transmitted through the eyes, anus, vagina, mouth, and wounds.

The type 1 infection causes most oral herpes contaminations, while the type 2 infection is answerable for most genital herpes. Since the tactile neurons express moderately hardly any major histocompatibility complex (MHC) 1 particle, the contaminated cells are wasteful at introducing viral antigens to circling lymphocytes.

Upgrades, for example, fever, passionate pressure, or feminine cycle, reactivate the infection and contaminations of the encompassing epithelial tissues. Initiation of the type 1 infection can result in rankles around the mouth that are incorrectly called mouth blisters.

Type 2 infections can cause genital bruises, yet individuals tainted with either type 1 or 2 infections frequently come up short on any clear indications.

Contaminations of type 2 infection, which is explicitly transmitted, represent a genuine danger to the children of tainted moms and can expand transmission of HIV, the infection that causes aids (Campbell Reece, 2008).

Chapter 4: Herpes Diagnosis Testing

Getting tested may be the only way to know for sure when you have herpes. When you have sores or additional symptoms of herpes, visit a nurse or doctor.

Do I have herpes?

You can't tell when you have herpes simply by how you look or feel. Like all STDs, the only path to know for certain when you have herpes is to get tested.

If you see sores on or about your genitals, get tested with a nurse or doctor once you can. So, it's vital that you find out exactly what's happening.

What happens throughout a herpes test?

When you have blisters or sores, your physician or nurse will gently and carefully have a sample of fluid through the sores having a swab and test drive it.

In the event that you don't have any sores, talk to your physician or nurse about whether a blood test for herpes is practical for you personally. But herpes tests aren't normally recommended if you don't have symptoms.

The thought of getting tested might seem scary, but make an effort to relax. STD testing is definitely a normal part to be a responsible adult and caring for your wellbeing.

Where may I get tested for herpes?

A community health clinic, medical department, or your neighborhood Planned Parenthood health center.

You need to be honest with your nurse or doctor to allow them to help you find out which tests are best for you personally. Don't feel embarrassed: Your physician is here to assist you, never to judge you.

Chapter 5: Signs and Symptoms of Herpes

There are many symptoms that are related to having herpes simplex virus although, at times, you might not show any symptoms even when you have it for a very long time.

However, many individuals show signs which are related to the ones that will be highlighted below:

- Pains in the affected body region especially the genitals, mouth, face, and rectum.
- Unable to urinate.
- Unappealing vaginal discharge that smells badly.
- Blisters on the skin with a change in color like red.
- Cold irritating sores in the mouth and lips.
- Illness and fever.
- Characteristic burning and tickling sensation in the genital region of both males and females.
- Swelling of the anus or rectum persists.
- Pains in the Muscle.
- Presence of blisters in the cervix.
- Lymph nodes become enlarged.
- Burning and itching in the affected area.
- Sores in the genital region.
- Presence of an ulcer immediately there is a breakage in the blister.
- Greater than normal temperature.
- Pain during urination.

Expression of Herpes Virus

Expression of herpes simplex virus is firstly expressed via mutation of prevailing viruses. RNA viruses have an abnormally increase percentage of mutation since mistakes in duplicating their RNA genomes are not altered by proofreading. Several mutations alter their prevailing viruses into fresh genetic variations that can cause disease, even in individuals who are resistant to the virus.

Further, the expression of herpes virus is secondly expressed via dispersal of herpes virus from a small isolated human populace. For instance, HIV was not noticed for several years before it starts to transmit worldwide. Thus, technological and social factors, including affordable international tourism, blood transfusions, unprotected sexual intercourse, and the abuse of injection of drugs, permitted a formerly uncommon human disease to become a worldwide problem.

Thirdly, the herpes virus is expressed via the transmission of the prevailing virus from other animals such as domestic and wild animals. It is reported that about three-quarters of fresh diseases that affect man is originated in this manner. Animals that carry and transmit viruses but are usually not affected by it are known to act as a natural reservoir for such virus disease. Hence, they are termed as a reservoir host. They do not show symptoms but when they transmit it to man it becomes symptomatic.

Common Symptoms of Herpes

Many people are carrying this virus without showing any symptoms, but some people have their signs and such people can develop them within 2–12 days after they are exposed to the virus.

However, whenever someone is exposed to the virus for the first time, the virus's recurrences tend to happen more frequently, but as time goes on, the remission periods get longer. Each occurrence of the virus tends to become less severe.

Primary Symptoms

The primary symptoms are those of someone who just gets exposed to the genital herpes experience, which is usually severe. The symptoms include:

- Blisters on the external genitalia like the cervix or vagina and sometimes, red blister on the skin.
- Just like the blister, there will be ulceration on the cervix or vagina.
- Experience vaginal discharge.
- Pain and itching on the vagina and cervix.
- The lymph nodes will become tender or enlarged
- Experience pain whenever urinating.
- Experience cold sores around or in the mouth.
- Experience high temperature (fever) or malaise.
- Some people's ulcers will get heal and will not suffer from any lasting scars.
- Experience frequent infection symptoms.

These symptoms don't last long and are not severe like in the primaries symptoms stage and don't last more than ten days.

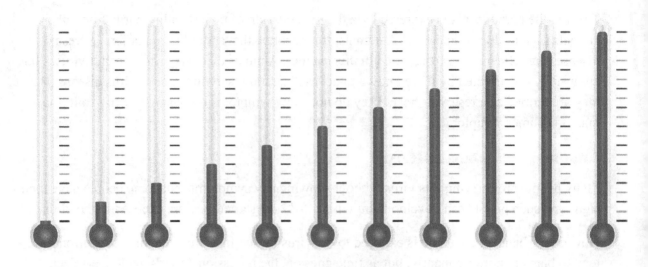

Chapter 6: The Herpes Virus Healing Method & Dr. Sebi

Method 1 – Curing Herpes via Dr. Sebi's Food Plan

Dr. Sebi frequently referred to that so one can heal the frame, one has first to cleanse the body, then feed it the nutrients it wishes. Dr. Sebi contends that "diseases" cannot live in an alkaline frame and so it's far vital to cleanse and alkalize the body to carry it to a more fit state.

Step 1 Smooth up the Machine

Detoxifying the gadget is pivotal to freeing the edge of ailments. To start with, we start with the guide of purging out the colon (entrails).

Colon cleanse

Use the chelation 2 for this. You can make your own if you can't buy it. There also are other techniques for cleaning the colon and cleansing out the bowel. Any appropriate colon cleanses recipe needs to assist.

Apple Onion Colon Cleanse Recipe

Preparation time: 10 Minutes

Cooking time: 5 Minutes

Serving: Devour approximately three to 4 ounces within the morning.

Ingredients:

- 1 Apple

- A trickle of pectin (the white part of the citrus. Whilst you peel an orange or lime, that white component you see)

- 1 Big onion

Direction:

1. Mix or blend together with water.

Nutrition:

- Calories 138

- Protein 2.1g

- Carbohydrate 35.3g

- Sugar 23.2g

- Fiber 5.7g

- Fat 0.1g

Step 2 Cleanse More to the Organs of the Body

The Viento is blanketed in Dr. Sebi's small cleaning package deal as it allows you to clean the frame at a mobile stage. You can make your very own Viento system. You can actually but cross instantly to step three.

Step 3 Easy and Nourish the Blood

The iron plus and bio Ferro will support to purify the blood, enhance move to the frame, and nourish the cells. As stated, you can purchase or make your very own—it's far very smooth to do that.

Dose: Take the spices as coordinated on the true framework.

Throughout this technique, the weight loss plan should be very mild, along with only alkalizing meals, often fruits and greens. Follow Dr. Sebi's nutritional manual, however, some items on the listing ought to no longer be fed on while one is trying to reverse extreme health conditions.

Matters on the listing to eat: Culmination, greens together with lettuce, mushrooms, lambs sector, dandelion greens, mustard vegetables, vegetables, amaranth vegetables and lettuce, coconut (jelly and water) natural teas, smoothies and juices.

Matters at the listing to avoid: avocados, oils, chickpeas, nuts (all), and grains (all).

Notice: Other than the teas, the entire thing otherwise you eat up should be all uncooked, for example uncooked. Purchase characteristic if suitable, if not, does the quality you can, and make certain suppers are washed appropriately before use.

Hydration: consume plenty of water to flush the system.

Bladderwrack/sea moss: Add the bladderwrack/sea moss aggregate to smoothies and have it in teas.

If cash is a huge issue, in phrases of being capable of affording the herbs, then move a chunk lighter at the herbs.

Begin by cleaning the bowel and changing the eating regimen to predominantly end result and greens, preferably one hundred% uncooked or as close as feasible.

Use the bromide powder (sea moss and bladderwrack) to make shakes and feature teas day by day.

Further, add the elderflower, burdock, dandelion, sarsaparilla, and ginger to your regimen. Integrate them to make teas.

Method 2 – Treating Herpes Via Water Fasting

Water fasting may be extraordinarily effective. It might be one of the easiest methods to rid the body of pathogens and pollutants, raise the immune gadget, and allow the frame to heal. It isn't always really helpful to begin water fasting rapidly without a preceding fasting incursion.

There are fasting clinics one ought to visit. I am aware that the numbers are increasing, lengthy status centers with suitable reputations are tangle wood wellbeing middle and true north wellness center (U.S. Based). It's not a reasonably-priced venture, such a lot of humans won't be able to come up with the money for the ride to a center.

But one doesn't need to go to a fasting center with the intention of rapid. If there are not any other extreme underlining health conditions, you could build up to a fast through preparing the frame (so to reduce the consequences of detox signs). Make sure you have a guide around you, together with a partner or buddy, and additionally, preferably someone with the revel in of fasting

Constructing up to Water Fast

- Start with three days of bowel cleanse.

- Consume a complete plant-based total food regimen for seven days.

- Do another effective 3-day bowel cleanse consuming uncooked culmination and greens for the duration of this period.

- Do a seven days' mono-rapid ideally on melon, grapes, mango, or apples.

- Follow up with a 3-day juice fast, mainly inexperienced juices and the juices of citrus culmination.

- Begin your water fast.

Reminder: It's far most popular for lengthy fasting tries to go to a fasting health center where you may have the understanding of individuals who can help you thru the difficult days beforehand. In case you aren't capable of going to a fasting health facility, then it might be vital to have help round you. If fasting on one's very own, it isn't advisable to move past 7-10 days.

Who Ought not to Fast

It isn't always recommended that some people go on a water fast, these encompass:

- Pregnant ladies.

- Those are handling anorexia.

- People laid low with debilitating diseases and have little energy.

- Those in advanced stages of diseases e.g. Cancers.

- Individuals who are affected by intense intellectual disorders that require professional treatment. If you are tormented by a less severe mental ailment, it's far essential to have support around you.

It is vital that the fast is broken successfully.

- Start with the handy juices, vegetable juices, non-sweet fruit juices. Have them for three consecutive days (assuming a 7 to ten days water rapid. The longer the water fasts, the slower and longer the re-feeding length).

- Have raw culmination for some other two days.

- Introduce mild raw salads.

- Slowly introduce other foods.

Note: Eat small food as wished, chunk foods well, pay attention to the frame's signals.

Method 3 – Via Juicing

After the initial bowel clean of at least three days, have handy juices and teas. This consists of inexperienced or vegetable juices specifically, you will have more of those at the start, then add fruit juices (citruses and melons).

- Constructing as much as a juice speedy

- Three days of colon cleanse.

- Seven days all raw culmination and greens.

- Begin juicing.

- Examine constipation.

The duration varies; set a minimum goal of 21 days. Take natural teas, such as those mentioned above, further growth water intake.

Tip: Gracefully taste your juices within the mouth earlier than swallowing.

Method 4 – Vain Water Fasting and Juicing

This is where water fasting and juicing are combined. With this approach, a deliberate sample is created consuming a balance of fruit juices and water.

- Blended water and juice plan

- Juice in the mornings

- Water within the days

- Juice at nights

Dr Sebi Final Curative Process of Herpes Virus

After you are done with the detoxification process, you are going to start with the use of curative herbs, which are loaded with high iron contents.

Dr Sebi recommended some of his products for the cure of the herpes virus. The product names are bromide plus powder, iron plus, bio ferro. You can use this product by following the directions: written on it by Dr Sebi. He also recommended certain herbs you can prepare yourself at home if you cannot buy the product.

There are about eleven (11) types of herbs Dr Sebi used for the cure of herpes. All the plants contain a rich source of potassium phosphate and iron. These herbs are listed below:

- Sarsaparilla.
- Sarsil berry.
- Guaco.
- Conconsa.
- Purslane.
- Kale.
- Dandelion.

- Lamb's quarters.
- Burdock.
- Blue vervain.
- Yellow dock.

Preparation of the Herbs

Ensure the plants are well dried and preserve in a dry and clean container. Grind the herbs into powder form.

Collect one tablespoon of each of the above plants and add four cups of spring water.

Place it in a source of heat and allow boiling.

The boiling should be done within 3 minutes or until you observe that the extracts of the plants are coming out and the color of the water changed.

Bring it out of the heat source and leave it for a few minutes to get cool before consumption, although herbs are best taken when hot because the bitterness will be reduced.

Take these herbs two times daily with a glass cup until your required result is achieved.

Blue Vervain

This plant is rich in iron, which is very good to prevent short of blood (anemia) in the body.

Sarsil Berry

This plant contains iron content because it is a berry from the plant of sarsaparilla. Dr Sebi spoke extensively on this plant and stressed its effectiveness for the cure of herpes.

Guaco Plant

This plant contains a high content of iron, strengthens the immune system, and also contains potassium phosphate that makes it effective against the herpes virus.

Sarsaparilla

This plant contains the highest iron component, and it is employed for the treatment of herpes simplex and genital herpes.

Researchers suggested that sarsaparilla has mechanisms that help to treat syphilis, herpes, rheumatic affections, passive general dropsy, and gonorrheal rheumatism.

The active ingredients present in this plant that makes it effective against herpes are triterpenes, sarsaparilloside, parillin, smitilbin, and phenolic compounds.

Conconsa

This plant is an African plant. The highest concentration of potassium phosphate is embedded in it, which fights against the herpes virus.

Purslane

Purslane contains a rich amount of iron content. The herbalist has stated that this plant is effective for treating herpes simplex.

Kale Plant

This plant is rich in iron antioxidants. It also contains more lysine, an amino acid ratio that's important to suppress the herpes virus. The amino acid lysine helps to inhibit the multiplication of herpes viral cells in the body.

- Yellow dock
- This plant is rich in iron.
- Lamb's quarters
- This plant is rich in iron.

Dandelion Root Effectiveness for Herpes

This plant is rich in iron and potassium. It is one of the most popular herbs that are essential for the healing of different illnesses. It has been used for the treatment of wounds on the skin. This plant is also an essential tool used for the treatment of liver abnormalities, which helps the cleansing and detoxification of toxic substances in the body.

Moreso, dandelion helps in the removal of stones in the kidney and the bladder. It helps in the lowering of high blood pressure levels.

This plant has been extensively used in alternative medicine for the treatment of hypertension, herpes, HIV/aids, urinary tract infection, breast cancer, skin infection, and hypoglycemia in many patients.

The active ingredients present in this plant are:

- Carotenoids.
- Taraxsterol.
- Asparagine.
- Choline.
- Tannins.
- Sterols.
- Araxacin.
- Triterpenes.

- Taraxol.

Scientific Proof of Dandelion for the treatment of Herpes

An exploration was completed at the Jiangxi medical college. They screened a few restorative spices against the sort 1 herpes simplex infection. After rehashed screens, dandelion was incorporated among the spices that are compelling against herpes.

Preparation of Dandelion for the Reversing Herpes Virus

- Collect the healthy root of the dandelion.
- Dry the plant with the use of direct sunlight. This should be done after you have perfectly rinsed the root.
- Grind the root into powder form.
- Collect 2 tbsp of the powder and boil in one cup of water.
- Drink this tea twice daily.

Before you begin the use of this plant for herpes and aids treatment, ensure you have initially undergone the 30 days detox process to enable you to clean the body at the intercellular and intracellular level.

The detoxing process will help clean the mucus membrane, which is found in the skin and the lymphatic system. This membrane protects the cells in the body.

Also, there are several products recommended by Dr Sebi for the treatment of Herpes if you do not want to use dandelion root. The products can be used together as instructed by Dr Sebi.

How to Treat Herpes with Dr Sebi's Diets on a Budget

Using Dr Sebi's diet to cure herpes is a straightforward and effective process. Dr Sebi's diets can help to eradicate the herpes simplex virus on a budget. To achieve this, you need to follow the following procedure:

Eat Alkaline Diets and Herbs

Following the alkaline plant-based diets is essential in healing the herpes virus. Following the alkaline diet means that you avoid starchy food and meats and only consume healthy fruits and vegetables.

Starchy foods and meats help to increase the herpes simplex virus. So, it is something you must have to avoid if you want to heal of herpes virus.

Following the recommended foods in Dr Sebi's diet list will help cleanse your body of any harmful substance fighting against your healing, improve your immune system, and replenish your body.

Intermittent Fasting and Herbs

It is also essential you practice intermittent fasting and take healthy herbs that can detoxify your body. Consume herbs with high iron content and herbs that contain the vital nutrients that your body needs to heal of the herpes virus. Dr Sebi recommended the intake of green juice with high iron content, the consumption of herbs, and water for detoxification.

General healthy guide

As much as possible, you should avoid processed and cooked foods, which are foods with high acid content. Practice intermittent fasting and take herbs and water. When you are done with fasting, eat healthy fruits and vegetables because they help accelerate your healing process. Continue taking the recommended Dr Sebi's foods even after healing to make the healing permanent. You don't need to spend a fortune on drugs and medications that don't work. All you need is to follow the doctor's Sebi recommended alkaline-based diet, and you will eradicate the herpes virus from your body.

The Most Effective Medical Herbs to Cure Herpes

For Dr Sebi's herbs for herpes to work effectively for you, you have to start with the cleansing herbs. Below are some of the cleansing herbs you need to take:

Cleansing Herbs

Mullein

Mullein helps to cleanse the lung and also helps to activate lymph circulation in your neck and chest. For throat, mouth, and respiratory problems, Mullein is taken orally. Traditionally, a dose of 4-5 grams of flowers (daily) is recommended. As for the leaves, the dose is 2-3 grams dried or 15-30 milliliters fresh.

Sarsaparilla Root

Sarsaparilla root helps to purify the blood and target herpes. Jamaican sarsaparilla roots are highly recommended because they are a great source of iron, and they are good for healing. Its cancer-healing properties are well-documented even in Western medicine. In powdered form, the dosage for this root is 0.3-2 grams daily. In dried form, the dosage is 1-4 grams.

Dandelion

Dandelion helps to cleanse the gallbladder and the kidney. Dandelion can be used in a multitude of ways, most notably as a tea or infusion. The daily recommended dosage is 2 to 8 grams of fresh dandelion or 3 to 4 grams of powdered dandelion root (mixed with 150 milliliters of water).

Chaparral

Chaparral helps to cleanse harmful heavy metals from your gallbladder and blood and also cleanse the lymphatic system.

Chaparral has been used for a range of medicinal uses throughout history but can be harmful when taken orally, even at low dosage, so consult an expert before using it.

Eucalyptus

You can use Eucalyptus to cleanse your skin through a sauna or steam. Dosage varies, but oral consumption is discouraged.

Guaco Herb

Guaco heals wounds, cleanses the blood, promotes perspiration, increases urination, keeps your respiratory system healthy, and improves digestion. Guaco is usually used as an extract, infusion, or syrup.

As an infusion, a ½-cup taken three times a day is recommended. As an extract, the dosage is 3-4 milliliters daily.

Cilantro

Cilantro is the name for the leaves of the coriander plant. Cilantro helps to remove heavy and harmful metals from your cells, and this is essential for the healing of herpes because the herpes virus hides behind your cell walls. Cilantro is conventionally cooked, and dosage varies depending on the user's need.

Burdock Root

Burdock root helps to cleanse the lymphatic system and the liver. Burdock can be eaten and can also be made into a tea or infusion. 6g per day as a root extract in tea is recommended, but not much information on the most appropriate dosage of burdock is currently available.

Elderberry

Elderberry helps to remove mucus from the lungs and upper respiratory system. One tablespoon of elderberry-based syrup is recommended for a good bodily cleanse, but the concentration of elderberry syrup may vary, so read the box's directions or consult an expert before using it.

Cleansing Herbs

Burdock Root

It is a natural diuretic that helps eliminate excess sodium in the body by increasing urine production and has excellent blood cleansing properties. It also helps detoxify the liver and strengthen the lymphatic system.

Dandelion

It is well known for its cleansing properties for the spleen, kidneys, and gallbladder. Besides that, it is also very rich in iron, calcium, and increases the production of bile to strengthen the immune system.

Sarsaparilla

It nourishes the body with its high iron content, thus helping to purify the blood. It was specifically recommended by Dr Sebi against herpes, skin diseases, and other venereal diseases. It is also good to know that the Indians of the Amazon used sarsaparilla to treat general weaknesses. If possible, get Jamaican Sarsaparilla.

Elderberry

It is known that the elderberry has diaphoretic and anti-catarrhal properties. Its main function is to remove mucus from the respiratory system. In fact, it is often used as a local anti-inflammatory agent for the respiratory tract to fight flu, colds, and sinusitis.

Mullein

It is very effective in cleansing the bronchial tubes and the lungs from mucus. It also soothes inflammations in the respiratory tract and helps to stimulate the lymphatic nodes in the neck and chest.

Chaparral

Chaparral has proven to have antibiotic, anti-inflammatory, and bactericidal properties. It will strengthen the lymphatic system, detoxify the gallbladder, and cleans heavy metals from the blood. It is considered a 'cure-all' by the Arizona Indians.

Note. The sale of Chaparral has been banned in the U.S. and UK because of reported cases of toxicity. It is not known if the individuals may have been taking other toxic substances in addition to chaparral, or how did they prepare it. Please consult your personal physician before taking it.

Guaco

Guaco is a strong natural diuretic that helps detoxify the blood, it is also well known to be a great natural bronchodilator, expectorant, and cough suppressant. It is highly recommended to drink lots of water while taking it to amplify its cleansing effects. In Africa and South America is often used as an antidote for venomous snake bites and diarrhea. Guaco leaves are also used to heal wounds and treat certain venereal diseases, they also have great pain reliever, antibacterial, and anti-inflammatory effects. It is very effective in expelling phlegm, but keep in mind that it will also thin the blood, which is beneficial for people affected by hypertension as well.

Cilantro

While some people do not put it on the approved product list, Dr Sebi himself often mentioned it in his speeches, which is why I wanted to add it to this list. It is highly recommended for herpes as the latter hides behind the cell walls, Cilantro helps to remove heavy and harmful metals from the cells, thus allowing the body to locate the virus and begin the healing process.

Cascara Sagrada

It is widely known as a strong stimulant laxative and pancreatic stimulant. More than 20% of the commercial laxatives are built up by using this herb. It acts upon the vasomotor system, increasing bowel movements and leading to relief of constipation. It is strongly recommended for chronic constipation, congestion of the liver, and torpor of the low bowel.

Revitalizing Herbs

Wakame

Wakame is one of the best natural choices against the herpes simplex virus.

A scientific study conducted on 15 patients with active herpes infection and 6 patients with latent herpes infection has proven that a proprietary preparation of Tasmanian wakame seaweeds (GFS extract) has inhibitory effects not only on the rooting of the virus in the human cells, but has also increased the healing rate of Herpetic onsets and has inhibited its reactivation.

The test was specifically targeted for HSV-1, HSV-2, and during the administering the subjects' human T cell mitogenicity and anti-Herpes activity were monitored.

Zataria Multiflora

Zataria Multiflora Boiss, also known as Zaatar in ancient Iranian medical books, is a plant from the family of Labiatae and very similar to thyme, which wildly grows in Afghanistan, Pakistan, and Iran. The plant is widely used by the Middle Eastern population in traditional folk remedies for its antibacterial, antiseptic, analgesic, and antiparasitic properties. A study conducted by the Islamic Azad University of Iran has proven that essential oils extracted from this plant have a significant inhibitory effect on HSV-1 and, therefore, could be used as an anti-HSV-1 agent in the context of herbal mouth wash.

Hyssopus Officinalis

A research study conducted by Mandana Behbahani, a biologist from the University of Isfahan in Iran, has shown that methanolic extract of the leaves of Hyssopus officinalis has exhibited impressive results against "both wild type and resistant strains of HSV".

She stated that when tested in vitro, the extract completely inhibited plaques formation of both of the two strains of HSV-1 with minimal cell cytotoxicity. When it was then tested in vivo, the extract significantly postponed the outbreak of HSV-1 infection by over 50%. It also increased the average survival time of infected mice by 55-65% compared to the non-treated mice. The mortality rate for mice treated with the extract was also significantly reduced by 90% in comparison with the non-treated mice that exhibited 100% mortality. This study suggests that Hyssopus extract is a powerful anti-viral agent against herpes simplex viruses and can be used as a remedy for HSV infections.

Pao Pereira

Pao Pereira is very effective against the HSV as not only it suppresses the virus, but it also inhibits the replication of the herpes simplex virus genome. It was also recommended by Sebi himself for a lot of different illnesses.

Pau d'Arco

Pau d'Arco's chemical constituents have demonstrated in vitro antiviral properties against herpes simplex virus type 1 & 2 as well as many other viruses such as vesicular stomatitis virus, influenza, poliovirus, and many others.

Oregano Essential Oil

This essential oil starts to be very effective as an antiviral at 90% concentrate, anything less than 90% is not really going to give you the benefit that you need to heal from the herpes virus.

Rub it to your lower spine, which is where the HSV stays dormant waiting to be triggered. It can also be applied under the tongue as well as to the genital area.

It is recommended to dilute it by putting 10 drops into two ounces of extra-virgin olive oil or coconut oil because it can burn your skin. Apply it two to three times per day.

Ginger Essential Oil

Ginger oil is very similar to oregano oil, it has the potential to kill the herpes virus on contact, but you must be careful and remember to dilute it with a carrier oil such as extra-virgin oil or coconut oil. Use the same ratios that were stated for oregano essential oil.

Sea Salt Bath

A bath with sea salt will help to absorb electrolytes through the skin and provide relief during the outbreak of the symptoms. So, fill a tub with warm water, put about a third or a half a cup of sea salt into the water, and make sure that it is completely dissolved and relax by soaking completely in it.

Holy Basil

This adaptogen is widely known for its effectiveness against adrenal fatigue and for increasing the sense of well-being.

Blue Vervain

Probably the most famous adaptogen on this list, blue vervain has proven to have antispasmodic, mild diaphoretic, and sedative properties. It has been used to fight depression, hysteria, stimulating the adrenal glands, and helping to relieve stress.

Astragalus

It provides support to the immunological system while bringing relief to the body in adapting to daily stress.

Gotu Kola

It is widely known in Ayurvedic medicine for its versatility in curing various types of illnesses. It is a powerful blood tonic, a detoxifier, an antibiotic, and a great adaptogen. It is used by Chinese herbal medicine to treat Parkinson's disease, rheumatism, and for recovery from surgical operations.

Chapter 7: FAQs about Dr. Sebi Cure for Herpes

1. Why Women Stand A Greater Risk Of Getting Infected With Genital Herpes?

One of the reasons is the way women are made. The genital area has a large number of mucosal cells, i.e., cells that contain body fluids.

Another reason is the menstrual cycle. This cycle change affects the immune system. A lower immune system makes it easier for the herpes virus to create an infection.

3. How Do Women Contact Genital Or Vaginal Herpes?

Women contact herpes just the same way men do. The fluids released by the HSV -1 and HSV -2 all contain the virus that causes herpes.

4. What Are The Parts Of Healings?

Whether it is arthritis, HIV or dementia, there are two necessary steps or parts to healing known as the cleansing/detoxifying of the body and revitalizing of the body.

5. What Are The Things To Consider For Healing Herpes?

There are three things that you need to consider for treating herpes. These things include: Build back your immune system: anyone suffering from herpes means that he is suffering from a weak immune system. So, the first thing to consider is how to build back the immune system to work correctly again. The food to consume: you need to consume more food that is mineral-rich like sea moss daily.

6. What Are The Best Food To Consume When Treating Herpes?

Some foods best suit someone that is treating herpes among the food list of Dr. Sebi. These foods include: Fruits and vegetables

Please note that intermittent fasting is essential for your healing, and you should try as much as you could to avoid nuts, grain and seed except for hempseed that you can consume as milk (hemp milk).

7. What Are The Food To Avoid While Treating Herpes?

Avoid eating inflammatory food like amino acid as amino acid helps in feeding the herpes virus, leading to a flare-up. She refined sugar b. Processed food c. Animal products (meat and dairy protein)

8. What Are The Habit To Eliminate?

It would help if you eliminated some little but essential habits, which is because of the toxic that such habit permits you to consume knowingly or unknowingly.

9. What Are The Ways To Stimulate The Lymphatic System?

To stimulate your lymph system, kindly get involved with the following:

Make sure you take a walk for at least 15 minutes daily. Alternatively, you can engage yourself on a daily exercise .Or jumping on a trampoline. Or engage in dry brushing

10. What Are The Basic System Or Structure That I Need To Cleanse To Heal Herpes?

Based on what late Dr. Sebi states, the only way to get rid of disease and live a sick-free life is by cleansing the following structure through intra-cellular cleansing. It doesn't matter what disease you want to get rid of, and the steps remain the same. That is, cleansing of:

a. Gallbladder b. Lymph gland c. Liver d. Kidney e. Colon and f. Skin

Chapter 8: Why Is Dr Sebi Treatment Successful

It is best because it works in herpes: This is the best treatment so far from the effectiveness point of view. There is very little effective herpes treatment around the globe. There are antiviral drugs that are expensive yet ineffective. They only give a fake feeling of wellness when, in fact, nothing is working as it should in your body. Despite the intake of antiviral drugs by some herpes patients, the herpes simplex virus still thrives without limitation. It is a lot of sacrifices to choose antiviral drugs over traditional medicines as the former only pamper the symptoms of herpes with many underlying side effects. Some other herbs are safe but do not produce the same effect as Dr. Sebi's cure. It makes Dr. Sebi's cure the only solution that is perfect for every herpes patient as nothing comes close to its healing prowess.

It is the best option because it is the only safe option: Dr. Sebi's cure is all-natural, and all the ingredients contained therein are devoid of any synthetic material. Herbs have been in existence since the time the very first man was made, and the reason they are still preferred over conventional medicine is that they have zero side effects. Since Dr. Sebi's cure is entirely made up of herbs, you do not have to worry about your present and future health. These herbs work like magic, not only in curing you of herpes but also in improving your health every day. Those who have used Dr. Sebi herpes cure in the past have backed up the claim that these herbs indeed improved their health as they felt more energetic after starting the course. This makes Dr. Sebi herpes cure the only alternative you should consider.

It is best because it is cost-effective, too: With antiviral drugs, you need a prescription. Dr. Sebi's herpes cure is different, as you do not need a prescription when you make a purchase. This alternative medicine tells you a lot of your money that goes into consultation. Health is essential, but the money being spent on antiviral drugs is exorbitant, but that does not guarantee their effectiveness. On the other hand, Dr. Sebi's herpes cure is available on naturalherpescure.org. You do not need to pay a consultation fee, and zero marketing cost is involved. You only pay for what you get. Since this drug is effective and gets the job done, you are not throwing away your hard-earned cash.

It is best because scientists certify it: Dr. Sebi's claim to cure herpes with herbs has been verified to be authentic by various medical and scientific researches. Some of the studies established more facts about the antiviral properties of the herbs used in the herpes cure. Natural antiviral properties can rid the body of the herpes virus without any side effects. In addition to the antiviral properties found in these herbs, they have also been found to be immune-modulatory. This means they directly boost the body's disease-fighting mechanism. A more muscular immune system means that the herpes simplex virus's replication can be put under control for every herpes patient to live a herpes free life. All the researches about Dr. Sebi herpes cure approve it as the best solution for herpes.

It is best because it gives you herpes free life: The efficacy of Dr. Sebi herpes cure is the sole reason it is considered the best herpes treatment worldwide. No other treatment has been verified to cure herpes, only this one can. You need to trust Dr. Sebi's methods to live a herpes free life.

The highlighted points are some of the reasons why Dr. Sebi herpes cure is the best one around. If you think it is time to put an end to the pains herpes is putting you through, you should give this cure a try. Before that, you must know the content of this cure. First and foremost is Giloy. Giloy came into limelight for its antipyretic properties, which match what is found in every antibiotic in the market. Years later, scientists realized that this herb relieves pain and enhances immunity. The goodness contained in Giloy makes Dr. Sebi herpes cure the best one for you. The next ingredients on the list are ayurvedically herbs purified powder of zinc and silver. These ingredients are strong enough to help the immune system kill off every foreign body in the immune system. These ingredients can also be found in drugs for life-threatening diseases like cancer. Now you know why these herbs are essential in the herpes cure. Next, these drugs mentioned above are herbal formulations like Punarnavadi mandoor and Triphala. These two are renowned for the proper functioning of the liver, kidney, and other vital organs in the body. Dr. Sebi's herpes cure contains herbs, purified minerals, and potent ayurvedic medicines in simple terms. A combination of these ingredients will give you a robust immune system capable of keeping your body safe from day-to-day infections.

A look at these ingredients already gives a ray of hope for every herpes patient as the prospect of them killing the herpes simplex virus is assured. It doesn't matter whether you are on antiviral drugs right now. You are not being asked to stop taking it, give this cure a try and see the goodness for yourself. When you buy this perfect blend of herbs from naturalherpescure.org, you get a permanent cure for your problem. Otherwise, you will have to live with it for the rest of your days. The choice is yours. If I were you, I would head over to naturalherpescure.org to get a pack of Dr. Sebi herpes cure.

Curing Herpes The Dr. Sebi Way On A Budget

To not have much money, you are a herpes patient, and you want to get rid of herpes, what do you do?

1. Fasting and herbs

You can decide to fast during the period of taking Dr. Sebi, on numerous occasions, mentioned the importance of iron healing. One would consume water, green juices, and herbs during this period.

2. An alkaline diet and herbs

An alkaline diet is essential for the whole process of herpes cure. On numerous occasions, Dr. Sebi stressed the vitality of avoiding what he terms "blood and flesh," that is, animal flesh, meats, fish, and starchy foods. When it comes to healing herpes, you need to go over and beyond by avoiding some of the foods on Dr. Sebi's list.

Why? You May Ask

This is simply because some foods have more healing factors than others. Dr. Sebi has always referred to his food list as "least detrimental" as the diet is alkaline based, and it cleanses the body. This is the sole reason why fasting boosts this healing method's effectiveness as it allows the body to break acid consumption and begin the cleansing process.

During this time, alkaline herbs should be consumed in a high quantity as it helps to cleanse and nourish the body and strengthen the immune system.

What Really Should You Do?

1. Stay away from cooked foods.

2. Eliminate all acid-forming foods.

3. Fast while taking only herbs and water.

4. Immediately after a fasting period, eat only fruits and vegetables contained Green juices from leafy green vegetables should be a top priority. The better your detoxification process, the quicker your healing experience. Primarily green juices from your leafy green vegetables. The less reliable the diet during cleansing and detoxification, the faster and usually more effective the healing experience.

5. After herpes must have been defeated, only eat foods from the nutritional guide.

How Long Does It Take To Cure Herpes?

According to Dr. Sebi, how long it takes for herpes to be cured is dependent on factors like weight, fluid, the toxicity of the body, and state of health. He further explained that as the level of health varies from one individual to the other, so will the period of healing vary.

How Committed Are You?

Detoxifying herpes from the body is no rocket science; the result of the detoxification process depends on the level of commitment. Getting rid of herpes is no easy task as the virus hides in the central nervous system's spinal cord for a very long time. The body has to wake up herpes from its dormancy to escort it out. The body must create a toxic environment for the herpes virus. It is the reason why an alkaline diet is compulsory.

Chapter 9: Alkaline Recipes for Herpes Cure

Cherry Tomato & Kale Salad

Preparation Time: 10 minutes

Cooking Time: 0 minutes

Servings: 2

Ingredients:

- 2 tbsps. Ranch dressing
- 2 cups organic baby tomatoes
- 1 bunch kale, stemmed, leaves washed and chopped

Directions:

1. Mix all the ingredients in a bowl.

2. Divide the salad equally in two servings dishes.

3. Serve.

Nutrition:

Calories: 58 kcal

Fat: 6.9g

Carbs: 1.6g

Protein: 1.1g

Radish Noodle Salad

Preparation Time: 10 minutes

Cooking Time: 0 minutes

Servings: 4

Ingredients:

- 2 cups cooked radish florets
- 1 roasted spaghetti squash
- 1 chopped scallion
- 1 tbsp. sesame oil
- 1 bell seeded pepper, cut into strips

- 2 tbsps. toasted sesame seeds
- 1 tsp. sea salt
- 1 tsp. red pepper flakes

Directions:

1. Start by preparing the spaghetti squash by removing the cooked squash with a fork into a bowl.

2. Add the radish, red bell pepper, and scallion to the bowl with the squash.

3. In a small bowl, mix the red pepper flakes, salt, and sesame oil.

4. Drizzle the mixture to top the vegetables. Toss gently to combine them.

5. Add the sesame seeds to garnish.

6. Serve.

Nutrition:

Calories: 112 kcal

Fat: 6g

Carbs: 6.4g;

Protein: 2.5g

Caprese Salad

Preparation Time: 5 minutes

Cooking Time: 0 minutes

Servings: 2

Ingredients:

- 1 sliced avocado
- 2 sliced large tomatoes
- 1 bunch basil leaves
- 1 tsp. sea salt
- 1 cup cubed jackfruit

Directions:

1. In a bowl toss all the salad ingredients to mix.

2. Add the sea salt to season.

3. Serve.

Nutrition:

Calories: 125 kcal

Fat: 10.1g

Carbs: 9.1g

Protein: 2g

Spicy Eggplant

Preparation time: 15 minutes

Cooking time: 5 minutes

Servings: 4

Ingredients:

- 1 eggplant, cut into 1-inch cubes
- ½ cup filtered alkaline water
- 1 cup tomato, chopped
- ½ tsp Italian seasoning
- 1 tsp paprika
- ½ tsp red pepper
- 1 tsp garlic powder
- 2 tbsp. extra virgin olive oil
- ¼ tsp sea salt

Directions:

1. Add eggplant and water into the instant pot.
2. Seal pot with lid and cook on manual high pressure for 5 minutes.
3. When finished, release pressure using the quick release method than open the lid. Drain eggplant well.
4. Add oil in instant pot and set pot on sauté mode.
5. Return eggplant in the pot along with tomato, Italian seasoning, paprika, red pepper, garlic powder, and salt and stir until combined.
6. Cook on sauté mode for 5 minutes. Stir occasionally.
7. Serve and enjoy.

Nutrition:

Calories 107
Fat 7.6 g
Carbohydrates 10.5 g
Sugar 5.6 g
Protein 1.9 g
Cholesterol 0 mg

Brussels Sprouts & Carrots

Preparation time: 10 minutes

Cooking time: 5 minutes

Servings: 6

Ingredients:

- 1 ½ lb. Brussels sprouts, trimmed and cut in half
- 4 carrots, peel and cut in thick slices
- 1 tsp olive oil
- ½ cup filtered alkaline water
- 1 tbsp. dried parsley
- ¼ tsp garlic, chopped
- ¼ tsp pepper
- ¼ tsp sea salt

Directions:

1. Add all ingredients into the instant pot and stir well.
2. Seal pot with lid and cook on manual high pressure for 2 minutes.
3. When finished, release pressure using the quick release method than open the lid.
4. Stir well and serve.

Nutrition:

Calories 73
Fat 1.2 g
Carbohydrates 14.5 g
Sugar 4.5 g
Protein 4.2 g
Cholesterol 0 mg

Cajun Seasoned Zucchini

Preparation time: 8 minutes

Cooking time: 2 minutes

Servings: 2

Ingredients:

- 4 zucchinis, sliced
- 1 tsp garlic powder
- 1 tsp paprika
- 2 tbsp. Cajun seasoning
- ½ cup filtered alkaline water
- 1 tbsp. olive oil

Directions:

1. Add all ingredients into the instant pot and stir well.
2. Seal pot with lid and cook on low pressure for 1 minute.
3. When finished, release pressure using the quick release method than open the lid.
4. Stir well and serve.

Nutrition:

Calories 130
Fat 7.9 g
Carbohydrates 14.7 g
Sugar 7.2 g
Protein 5.3 g
Cholesterol 0 mg

Fried Cabbage

Preparation time: 10

Cooking time: 3 minutes

Serve: 6

Ingredients:

- 1 head cabbage, chopped
- ½ tsp chili powder
- ½ onion, diced
- ½ tsp paprika
- 1 onion, chopped
- 1 cup filtered alkaline water
- 2 tbsp. olive oil
- ½ tsp sea salt

Directions:

1. Add olive oil into the instant pot and set the pot on sauté mode.
2. Add onion in olive oil and sauté until softened.
3. Add remaining ingredients and stir to combine.
4. Seal pot with lid and cook on high pressure for 3 minutes.
5. When finished, release pressure using the quick release method than open the lid.
6. Stir well and serve.

Nutrition:

Calories 75
Fat 4.9 g
Carbohydrates 8 g
Sugar 4.2 g
Protein 1.7 g
Cholesterol 0 mg

Tofu Curry

Preparation time: 10 minutes

Cooking time: 4 hours

Servings: 4

Ingredients:

- 1 cup firm tofu, diced
- 2 tsp garlic cloves, minced
- 1 onion, chopped
- 8 oz. tomato puree
- 2 cups bell pepper, chopped
- 1 tbsp. garam masala
- 2 tbsp. olive oil
- 1 tbsp. curry powder
- 10 oz. coconut milk
- 1 ½ tsp sea salt

Directions:

1. Add all ingredients except tofu in a blender and blend until smooth.
2. Pour blended mixture into the instant pot.
3. Add tofu in a pot and stir well to coat.
4. Seal pot with lid and select slow cook mode and set the timer for 4 hours.
5. Stir well and serve.

Nutrition:

Calories 326
Fat 27.1 g
Carbohydrates 18.5 g
Sugar 9.7 g
Protein 8.9 g
Cholesterol 0 mg

Whole Cauliflower with Gravy

Preparation time: 10 minutes

Cooking time: 15 minutes

Servings: 5

Ingredients:

- 1 large cauliflower head, cut bottom leaves

For marinade:

- 1 tsp paprika ½ tbsp. olive oil
- tbsp. fresh parsley, chopped
- 1 tbsp. fresh thyme
- 3 garlic cloves
- Pepper
- Salt

For gravy:

- ½ tbsp. lime juice
- ½ tsp thyme
- 1 ½ cups filtered alkaline water
- 2 garlic cloves
- 1 tsp olive oil
- 1 onion, diced

Directions:

1. In a small bowl, mix together all marinade ingredients.
2. Rub marinade evenly all over cauliflower head.
3. For gravy: add oil in instant pot and set the pot on sauté mode.
4. Add garlic and onion in olive oil and sauté until onion is softened.
5. Add water, lemon juice, and thyme and stir well.
6. Place trivet in the instant pot. Place cauliflower head on a trivet.
7. Seal pot with lid and cook on manual high pressure for 3 minutes.
8. When finished, allow to release pressure naturally for 5 minutes then release using a quick release method.
9. Transfer cauliflower head to an oven-safe dish and broil for 3-4 minutes.
10. Puree the instant pot gravy using an immersion hand blender until smooth.
11. Set instant pot on sauté mode and cook gravy for 3-4 minutes.
12. Serve cauliflower with gravy.

Nutrition:

Calories 79
Fat 2.7 g
Carbohydrates 12.7 g

Sugar 5.1 g

Protein 3.9 g

Cholesterol 0 mg

Avocado Power Salad

Preparation Time: 10 minutes

Cooking Time: 0 minutes

Servings: 2

Ingredients:

- 1 cubed avocado
- 1 cup cooled cooked quinoa
- 1 tbsp. freshly squeezed Seville orange juice
- 1 tsp. sea salt
- 1 tbsp. onion powder
- 1 tbsp. onion powder
- 1/4 cup chopped cilantro
- 1 cup peeled and diced cucumber
- 1 cup halved cherry tomatoes
- 5oz. fresh and roughly chopped kale

Directions:

1. Mix all the ingredients.

2. keep the mixture in the fridge to chill for about 15 minutes

3. Serve.

Nutrition:

Calories: 433 kcal

Fat: 14.8g

Carbs: 63.6g

Protein: 13.7g

Roasted Vegetables

Preparation Time: 10 minutes

Cooking Time: 15 minutes

Servings: 2

Ingredients:

- 1-pint cherry tomatoes
- 2 cups chopped asparagus
- 1/2 cup halved mushrooms
- 1 tsp. sea salt
- 1 tbsp. onion powder
- 1 tbsp. coconut oil
- 1 seeded and chopped red bell pepper
- 1 peeled zucchini, cut into small bite-size pieces

Directions:

1. Adjust the temperature of your oven to 425° F.

2. In a bowl, mix all of the ingredients as you evenly coat the vegetables.

3. Transfer the vegetables into a baking pan.

4. Roast the vegetables for about 15 minutes until the vegetables are tender.

5. Serve.

Nutrition:

Calories: 132 kcal

Fat: 7.3g

Carbs: 15.4g

Protein: 2.9g

Summer Lettuce Salad

Preparation Time: 5 minutes

Cooking Time: 0 minutes

Servings: 4

Ingredients:

- 2 cups halved cherry tomatoes
- 4 cups romaine lettuce or iceberg
- 1 peeled and sliced cucumber
- 2 thinly sliced radishes

- 1 sliced scallion
- 1/2 cup shredded zucchini
- 14 oz. can have drained whole green beans

Directions:

1. Add all of the salad ingredients in a large bowl then toss with 2 tbsps. of the dressing.

2. Serve.

Nutrition:

Calories: 39 kcal

Fat: 0.3g

Carbs: 9g

Protein: 1.6g

Conclusion

Many people experience an overwhelming flood of feelings following their diagnosis. At first they may experience shock or disbelief accompanied by shame and sadness. With time, many people are capable to move into acceptance, however they may still be followed around by the nagging doubt that it is one way or the other their fault and that there is no permanent solution accessible to them. The luckiest among us are able to regain their self-confidence and the peace of understanding that their herpes diagnosis does not have to define or change them. But there is more out there! The herpes simplex virus is a very common infection, as you well know by now. As common as it is, the common scientific community nevertheless believes that there is no cure for this disease. However, if you do a little bit of digging for yourself as well as treat yourself with the help of this guide, you will prove yourself and discover that there is lots of evidence to suggest otherwise. Learning to cope with your herpes diagnosis is still a big step in the restoration process, but that doesn't have to be the place your experience ends. In analyzing this book you have acquired a wealth of understanding about the herpes simplex virus, its consequences on the human body, and common remedy methods. You have also learned the reality about what your health practitioner did now not tell you about this disease. While many people with herpes assume that it is a lifelong illness, there is a light at the end of the tunnel. By following the protocol outlined in this book you can heal your body from the herpes virus and experience the freedom of long-term relief.

HOW TO GET RID OF THE LIFE-CHANGING CHRONIC DISEASES NATURALLY USING DR. SEBI'S OFFICIAL TREATMENTS -2021 EDITION

Table of Contents

INTRODUCTION..4

CHAPTER 1: DR. SEBI AND HIS PHILOSOPHY 6

    Dr. Sebi's Treatment Philosophy 6

CHAPTER 2: DR. SEBI TEACHING AND METHODS......................8

    Principles 8

    Methodology 8

    Nutrition Guide 9

    DR. SEBI'S NUTRITIONAL FOOD LISTS 9

        The Doctor Sebi Diet Is Safe? 10

        Rules To Follow 11

CHAPTER 3: BENEFITS OF DR. SEBI TREATMENTS 13

CHAPTER 4: CANCER TREATMENT....................................19

    DR. SEBI'S MAGIC APPROACH FOR PROSTATE CANCER 19

    DR. SEBI RECOMMENDED HERBAL ITEMS FOR PROSTATE AND BREAST CANCER 20

    DR. SEBI GOOD TO DO IT YOURSELF................................20

    PREPARATION OF DR. SEBI DOSAGE FOR CANCER 21

    DR. SEBI HERBAL REMEDY FOR PROSTATITIS 22

CHAPTER 5: DIABETES TREATMENT.................................27

    ALKALINE DIET BENEFITS FOR DIABETICS 27

    DIABETICS ACID-ALKALINE FOOD CHART 27

    DIABETICS TOP BEST AND TOP WORST FOODS........................28

    DR. SEBI'S NUTRITION THAT CUTS OUT THE SUGAR 30

    DR. SEBI HERBAL SUPPLEMENTS FOR TYPE 2 DIABETES 31

    ROOT VEGETABLES AND FRUITS FOR DIABETICS 32

CHAPTER 6: CHRONIC DISEASE (KIDNEY) TREATMENTS 34

    INGREDIENTS IN THE KIDNEY DISEASE KIT............................34

        UTI Special Mix 34

        Kidney Stone Hunter 34

AHP Zinc Powder 35

Swarna Bang Tablets 35

Chandanadi Tablets 35

Punarnava Special Kidney Mix 35

CURE FOR KIDNEY PROBLEMS IN DR. SEBI'S WAY 35

TREATMENT AND PASSAGE OF KIDNEY STONES 36

HERBS USED FOR THE TREATMENT AND EJECTION OF KIDNEY STONES 36

CONSTITUENTS AND SCIENTIFIC BACKUP OF KIDNEY STONE REMOVAL HERBS 37

CHAPTER 7: HIV/STD TREATMENT **41**

CHAPTER 8: LUPUS TREATMENT **45**

DR. SEBI'S CURE FOR LUPUS 48

SUPPORT AND COPING 51

CHAPTER 9: VITAMINS & SUPPLEMENTS **52**

Supplements 52

RECOMMENDED ADDITIONAL SUPPLEMENTS 54

Vitamin B-12 54

Protein 54

Omega-3 Fatty Acids 55

CONCLUSION **56**

Introduction

Dr. Sebi (Alfredo Darrington Bowman) was a Natural therapist, Herbalist, and Biochemist. He is the founder of the USHA research institute, also known as the healing village.

Dr. Sebi employed the use of natural alkaline foods and herbs to cure various acute and chronic diseases. Doctor Sebi produces several medications and, in turn, used these medications to prevent and treat several diseases.

He ended up disappointed with Western scientific practices in treating his allergies, diabetes, and impotence. He goes to see an herbalist in Mexico whom Bowman claimed healed him. After that, Bowman started his very private recuperation exercising in Honduras. He evolved a treatment that he called the "African Bio-Electric Cell Food Therapy," and claimed that it could remedy a wide variety of illnesses, inclusive of most cancers and AIDS, in addition to an expansion of continual conditions and highbrow ailments. He additionally advanced related natural products. Bowman set up middle within the Eighties near La Ceiba, Honduras, and marketed his natural products in the United States.

He called his middle the USHA Research Institute, placed inside the village of Usha. He began to make use of foods that are rich in alkaline to treat various ailments.

The diseases he cures are numerous. Examples are arthritis, lupus, cancer, diabetes, leukemia, AIDS, asthma, impotence, eczema, epilepsy, fibroids, heart disease, hypertension, inflammation, lupus, multiple sclerosis, sickle cell …and many others.

He made the whole wide world in a free state in which those that are suffering from depressive illnesses obtained freedom from those illnesses and are living a healthy and happy life today.

Many dieters and alkaline food lovers are enjoying their health today because of the employment of Dr. Sebi's alkaline diets and herbs. They, therefore, declared that his diet had improved their wellbeing.

This African in Honduras grows to be recognized to have been married many times and had 17 children. His ideas on the muse of sickness germ idea and factored in fake-Afrocentric claims about Africans' first-rate generic traits and their diaspora.

Many African Americans argue that every time one tries to discover an option to the troubles of black people in the United States of America, they right now turn out to be the goal of attacks that commonly cause their deaths.

Several conspiracy theories have considering the fact that emerged following the taking photos of the 33-yr-old rapper, although different reviews allege that the taking pictures may have been gang-related.

Many humans, who include celebrities, believe that Hussle changed into killed because of his work highlighting the accomplishments and instances surrounding the death of famous herbal healer, Alfredo Bowman. Otherwise referred to as Dr. Sebi, Bowman died after claiming to have cured more than one sufferer of sicknesses of AIDS, diabetes, herpes, among others, strictly from natural treatments.

Sebi, who furnished schooling and healing for extra than 40 years, was at the center of numerous criminal complaints earlier than his "mysterious demise." During his early years, many claimed that the medical enterprise wanted to sideline him and his achievements.

Chapter 1: Dr. Sebi and His Philosophy

The man behind the Dr. Sebi Diet is Alfredo Bowman. He is a Honduran self-proclaimed herbalist and healer who uses food to improve health. Although he is already deceased, he has a number of followers in the 21st century. Because of his holistic approach, he has claimed to cure many kinds of diseases using herbs and a strict vegan diet. He has set up a treatment center in his home country before moving to New York City, where he has continued his practice and extended his clienteles from Michael Jackson, John Travolta, Eddie Murphy, and Steven Seagal, to name a few.

Although he calls himself Dr. Sebi, he does not hold any medical nor Ph.D. degree. Moreover, the diet has claimed to cure different conditions such as sickle-cell anemia, lupus, leukemia, and HIV-AIDS. This led to a lot of issues, particularly that he was practicing medicine without a license and his exorbitant claims. While he was charged for practicing without a license, he was acquitted in the early 1990s due to a lack of evidence. However, he was instructed to stop making claims that his diet can treat HIV-AIDS. While there are controversies that surround his name, there are so many benefits of his alkaline vegan diet that it is still popular even to this date.

Dr. Sebi's Treatment Philosophy

Agreeably, the way we eat is far different from that of our great ancestors. They base their Diet on plant and animal foods. The presentation of agriculture has altered our style of eating drastically. For instance, we have served grains. Using salt and sugar, and the use of meat, have increased. Also, individuals embraces cheddar, milk, and other milk items. All these foods produce a certain amount of acid in the blood after the body processes, absorb and metabolize them. This just infers that our Diet has become increasingly acid-delivering. We make dreadful decisions by choosing last the fruits and vegetables containing no or minimal acid. Dr. Sebi's Alkaline Diet exists on the reason that our eating habits must be alkaline. This means that our blood should maintain its normal pH level, which ranges from 7.35 to 7.45. Advertisers of the Alkaline Diet assume that the use of acid-creating foods breaks this harmony and causes essential supplements, such as calcium, potassium, sodium, and magnesium to vanish. Because of this, individuals become progressively defenseless to diseases. An acid-shaping diet exhausts the amount of catalyst in the body and decreases the levels of nerve energy. When chemical store diminishes, poor processing will probably happen. Thus, the minerals and nutrients necessary for ideal performance, quality, and health are not there. Similarly, the alkaline stores in the tissues and bones are spent hence, making you increasingly vulnerable to tissue and bone-related wounds or health conditions. Aside from these, an acid-delivering diet results in an increased uric acid level, which may shape uric crystals. These crystals can get pain and the inflammation of the joints that form into bursitis or arthritis.

Chapter 2: Dr. Sebi Teaching and Methods

Principles

Dr. Sebi felt the Western solution to illness was unsuccessful. He held that acidity and mucus — for starters, bacteria, and viruses — induced sickness.

A big dietary hypothesis is that illness can exist only in acidic conditions. In order to avoid or eliminate the disease, the purpose of the diet is to maintain alkaline conditions in the body. The official website of the diet offers botanical medicines helping to detoxify the body.

The platform does not relate any literature that supports its safety advantage claims. The Commission states that the Food and Drug Administration (FDA) has not studied the statements. Many behind the web understand that they are not professional practitioners and do not intend to provide professional recommendations.

Methodology

Often, stretching for the additional mile, you get to the areas you had only dreamed about. Going well on an alkaline diet will be the battle that ultimately contributes to a balanced lifestyle. An alkaline diet is an assumption that certain products, such as berries, vegetables, roots, and legumes, leave an alkaline residue or ash behind in the body. The body is strengthened by the key ingredients of rock, such as calcium, magnesium, titanium, zinc, and copper. The avoidance of asthma, malnutrition, exhaustion, and even cancer is an alkaline diet. Here are ten strategies to adopt the alkaline diet effectively.

1. Drink water - Water is probably our body's most important (after oxygen) resource. Hydration in the body is very important as the water content determines the body's chemistry. Drink between 8-10 glasses of water to keep the body well hydrated (filtered to cleaned).
2. Avoid acidic drinks like Tea, coffee, or soda - Our body also attempts to regulate the acid and alkaline content. There is no need to blink in carbonated drinks as the body refuses carbon dioxide as waste!
3. Breathe - Oxygen is the explanation that our body works, and if you provide the body with adequate oxygen, it should perform better. Sit back and enjoy two to five minutes of slow breaths. Nothing is easier than you can perform Yoga.

4. Avoid food with preservatives and food colors - Our body has not been programmed to absorb such substances, and the body then absorbs them or retains them as fat, and they do not damage the liver. Chemicals create acids, such that the body neutralizes them either by generating cholesterols or blanching iron from the RBCs (leading to anemia) or by extracting calcium from bones (osteoporosis).

5. Avoid artificial Sweeteners - These sweeteners, which tend to be high in low fat, are potentially detrimental to the body. In addition, Saccharin, a primary ingredient in sweeteners, triggers cancer. Keep away from these things, therefore. Go for less healthy food, still a decent one.

6. Exercise- The alkaline and the acidic element will also be matched. This is not just a question of consuming alkaline milk. A little acid (because of muscles) often regulates natural bodywork.

7. Satiate your urges for a snack by eating vegetables, or soaked nuts - Whenever we are thirsty, we still consume a little fast food. Establish a tradition of consuming fresh vegetables or almonds, even walnuts.

8. Eat the right mix of food - The fats and proteins of carbohydrates need a specific atmosphere when digested. And don't eat it all at once. Evaluate the nutritional composition and balance it accurately to create the best combination of all the nutrients you consume.

9. You can use green powders as substitutes for food - This tends to improve the alkaline quality of the body.

10. Sleep well, remain calm and composed even when under stress - Seek to escape the pain. Our mind regulates the digestive system, and only when in a relaxed, focused condition can you realize it functions properly. Relax, then, and remain safe!

Nutrition Guide

Dr. Sebi's Nutrition Guide includes a variety of guidelines, such as:

- Only eat nourishments recorded in the guide;
- Drink 1 gallon of common spring water day by day;
- Avoid creature items, half and half nourishments, and liquor;
- Avoid utilizing a microwave, which will "slaughter your food;"
- Avoid canned and seedless natural products.

Dr. Sebi's Nutritional Food Lists

Dr. Sebi's nutritional food lists are listed below:

Vegetable Diets

Izote flower and leaf, Kale, Mushrooms except for Shitake, Bell Pepper, Chayote, Cherry and Plum Tomato, Dulse, Garbanzo Beans, Arame, Wild Arugula, Avocado, Cucumber, Dandelion Greens, Amaranth, Watercress, Tomatillo, Turnip Greens, Wakame, Lettuce, Olives, Purslane Verdolaga, Squash, Okra, Hijiki, Nopales, Nori, Zucchini and Onions.

Fruit Diets

Peaches, Orange, Soft Jelly Coconuts, Cantaloupe, Prickly Pear, Cherries, Prunes, Bananas, Dates, Figs, Plums, Grapes, Apples, Pears, Limes, Mango, Berries, Raisins, Papayas, Melons, and Currants.

Alkaline Grains Diets

Kamut, Tef, Wild Rice, Spelt, Fonio, Amaranth, Quinoa, and Rye.

Alkaline Sugar Items

- Date Sugar.

- Agave Syrup from cactus (100% Pure).

Herbs Item

Dill, Onion powder, Basil, Pure sea salt, Oregano, and Cayenne.

Spices and Seasoning Diets

Dill, Achiote, Habanero, Savory, Basil, Thyme, Pure Sea Salt, Bay Leaf, Cayenne, Sweet Basil, Cloves, Onion Powder, Sage, Oregano, Powdered Granulated Seaweed, and Tarragon.

Herbal Tea Items

Elderberry, Tila, Burdock, Ginger, Fennel, Red Raspberry, Chamomile

The Doctor Sebi Diet Is Safe?

Research suggests, however, that a diet focused on plants will improve wellbeing. There are other issues that we will address in the following segment.

Other health benefits of herbal diets can include:

- Loss of weight -in the 2015 report, a vegan diet contributed to greater loss of weight than other, less restricted diets. After six months, participants lost up to 7.5 percent of their body weight on a vegan diet.

- Appetite management — A 2016 analysis of young male participants showed that after consuming a meal containing peas and beans, they feel more relaxed and happier than after a meal containing beef.

- Microbiome modification – the word "microbiome" generally applies to intestinal microorganisms. A research study in 2019 showed that a plant-based diet could favorably modify the microbiome and contribute to lower disease risk. However, more work would be required to validate this.

- Decreased risk of illness — A plant-based diet study in 2017 found that the potential for coronary heart failure may be lowered by 40 percent and the likelihood of developing metabolic syndrome and type 2 diabetes by around half.

Dr. Sebi's lifestyle encourages people to consume natural foods and removes packaged products. A 2017 study showed that a decrease in the consumption of refined foods would increase the overall nutritional consistency of the U.S. diet.

Dr. Sebi's diet is stringent and does not contain adequate significant nutrients that are not explicitly identified on the diet webpage.

If a person follows the diet, he or she may benefit from a healthcare provider who can advise on appropriate supplements.

Rules To Follow

To follow Dr. Sebi's diet, you must strictly adhere to his rules present on his website. Here is a list of his guidelines below:

- Do not eat or drink any product or ingredient not mentioned in the approved list for the diet. It is not recommended and should never be consumed when following the diet.

- You have to drink almost one gallon (or more than three liters) of water every day. It is recommended to drink spring water.

- You have to take Dr. Sebi's mixtures or products one hour before consuming your medications.

- You can take any of Dr. Sebi's mixtures/products together without any worry.

- You need to follow the nutritional guidelines stringently and punctually take Dr. Sebi's mixtures/products daily.

- You are not allowed to consume any animal-based food or hybrid products.

- You are not allowed to consume alcohol or any kind of dairy product.

- You are not allowed to consume wheat, only natural growing grains as listed in the nutritional guide.

- The grains mentioned in the nutritional guide can be available in different forms, like pasta and bread, in different health food stores. You can consume them.

- Do not use fruits from cans; also, seedless fruits are not recommended for consumption.

- You are not allowed to use a microwave to reheat your meals.

Chapter 3: Benefits of Dr. Sebi Treatments

Dr. Sebi's Diet is not just another fad. It has numerous benefits besides weight loss. Let's find out how following this vegan, alkaline-based approach to food will completely change our lives.

Weight Loss

As Hippocrates, the father of medicine, said eating healthy foods must be our primary goal. Not only bacteria and poisons are responsible for diseases, but irrational eating too.

Eating healthy foods should not be a privilege, but a way of life for all of us. If we eat what we crave for, it doesn't mean it is OK. If we eat what is good for us, then we are on the right path to well-being.

Weight loss is the main goal for most of us. Even if Dr. Sebi did not develop this diet for weight loss, we realize that we can lose weight by following his rules.

The diet is centered on eating vegetables and fruits, which are high in vitamins, minerals, fiber, and other compounds associated with reduced inflammation, oxidative stress, and protection against many diseases.

A study has shown that those who ate seven or more servings of fruits and vegetables a day had a lower incidence of cancer and heart disease.

This diet is based on principles opposite to the Western diet since it restricts us from processed foods, dense fats, sugar, salt, and other harmful ingredients.

Unfortunately, in the US, 42,4% of adults and 17% of children are obese. The numbers keep growing each year. Obesity leads to coronary artery diseases, cancer, strokes, type 2 diabetes, and death.

So we should take a stand and fight it as much as we can. Indeed, our society is not helpful at all. Think of all commercials, all sideboards with juicy snacks and juicy meats all around us, all TV shows with skinny actors, being bullied at school for an extra pound! It's not easy, but you should give it a try. Picture yourself in a past era, when people stood by each other, shared the little food that was on the table, the crops of a poor land occasionally. But what a great taste with the right people around you!

Tell me honestly, if it wasn't much better? Let go of the materialism that we are so famous for these days! Go back to your ancestor's way of living and eating! You will find it quite pleasurable.

Let's turn to facts! With this diet, you will lose an average of 26.6 pounds in six months. Studies have shown that!

As with any diet, it is best to talk to your general practitioner first. He will make sure to let you know if there is some health issue that will not allow you to follow this diet.

Furthermore, following this diet with foods low in calories (except for oils, seeds, avocado, and nuts) will never lead to a surplus of calories, even if you eat a large volume. So, it will only lead to weight loss and never weight gain.

Skeptics claim that it is not sustainable due to calorie restriction. Once you return to your old eating habits, you are bound to regain the weight you lost. On the other hand, if we make it a lifelong habit, it will provide us with long-term benefits, not only for weight loss but also for other aspects.

Detox

The Dr. Sebi Diet is also suitable for eliminating toxins and processed elements from the body.

Our body needs food, and we find all the food we need in nature. But some elements of the foods we eat are harmful. Once they are processed, some become toxic for our bodies. Consuming meats, some vegetables, dairy products, processed foods, and others leads to release of certain harmful elements. These are only a shortcut to chronic diseases.

The purpose of the Dr. Sebi Diet is to eliminate toxins bound to increase the risk of developing such diseases. It will also help us improve our health, vitality, and strength.

Intra-cellular cleansing is necessary to cleanse the body's systems on a cellular level to correct any damage or imbalances. Imbalances refer mainly to nutritional deficiencies and damages to your natural biological structure due to excess toxins, acids, calcification, and mucus build up in your body's systems.

Good Eating Habits

We are vegetarians, even if nobody tells you that. Mother Nature has a way to provide us with all we need. She takes care of plants, animals, and humans. For Amerindians, it represents the goddess of fertility who presides over planting and harvesting.

If nature didn't make it, don't take it!

Anyway, changing your eating habits is not easy, but you will find that it is quite easy if you follow some simple rules for some days. From there on, it will go naturally!

Lower Risk Of Chronic Diseases

A potential benefit of this diet is a lower risk of cancer, high blood pressure, heart diseases, and type-2 diabetes. Why? All due to natural foods that contain no harmful nutrients.

Some of the chronic diseases we can cure with Dr. Sebi's diet are:

1.   **Hypertension/ High blood pressure**

Hypertension is a medical condition in which blood pressure is insistently elevated. It is a major risk factor for strokes, heart failure, vision loss, and even dementia.

For the cure, we must keep away from meat and alcohol, drink not too much tea, and eat fruits and vegetables approved by Dr. Sebi. The vegetables to eat are olives, wild rice, lettuce, cucumber, bell peppers, kale, squash, valerian, and chickpeas. Dry fruits are the best choice for our diet.

2.   Type-2 diabetes

Type-2 diabetes is a chronic ailment that occurs as a result of obesity, especially in people over the age of 40. It is characterized by a lack of insulin, which is a crucial factor for digestion.

To cure diabetes, we must stay away from fried foods, teas with sugar, rice, and lens. The vegetables to eat are kale, cucumber, lettuce, cherry and plum tomatoes, chickpeas, bell peppers, squash, mushrooms, dandelion, and onions.

We can only eat fruits like red raspberry, plums, apples, and seeded key limes.

Sour soups are highly indicated for the cure of type-2 diabetes.

3.   Obesity

Obesity is a chronic disease in which excess body fat accumulated leads to various conditions, such as type-2 diabetes, cardiovascular diseases, obstructive sleep apnea, osteoarthritis, depression, and even some types of cancer.

It is caused by bad eating habits, sedentary lifestyle, genetics, gut flora, mental illnesses, and social determinants.

The best cure for obesity is eating fruits and vegetables, keeping away from meat and alcohol, and drinking plenty of liquids.

4.   Stress ulcer

An ulcer is a discontinuity in the body membrane, which hinders the normal function of the affected organ. Stress ulcer is the most common type of ulcer encountered in all countries.

It affects mainly the stomach and may lead to ulcerative perigastritis, stenosis, and massive bleeding.

Dr. Sebi's cure includes eating vegetables like tomatoes and squash, ripe fruits (apples, peaches, raisins), sour soups, and plenty of herbal teas, especially fennel and chamomile, for their soothing effect.

5.   Constipation

Constipation is a disorder that profoundly affects our well-being. Abdominal pain, bloating, and infrequent bowel movements may lead to other complications, such as hemorrhoids and anal fissure.

Digestion and metabolism help us get the nutrients we need and get rid of harmful elements. If they remain in our intestines too long, they will eventually become destructive.

Dr. Sebi's cure consists of eating fruits (mainly apples, peaches, plums, figs), vegetables (squash, kale, and chickpeas), basil, nuts, and plenty of herbal teas, especially fennel, dandelion, and chamomile.

6.   Atherosclerosis

Atherosclerosis is a syndrome in which the arteries narrow, and that may lead to strokes, coronary artery disease, and kidney problems.

Smoking and consumption of alcohol are forbidden. Coffee should be limited, but lettuce tea is a valid help.

In addition to physical exercise, we should eat wild rice, fruits, and vegetables.

7.   Herpes and STDs

Herpes and all STDs are viral infections that can not be defeated by the immune system.

The only means of prevention is safe sex. Dr. Sebi's cure includes herbal teas such as burdock and dandelion, eating a lot of dates, and lettuce.

8.   Gout

Gout is inflammatory arthritis characterized by recurrent intense pain, red, hot, and swollen joints, due to low uric acid levels in the blood. It may lead to kidney disease.

In this case, we should combine fiber with the uric acid in the digestive tract, so it does not form crystals deposits anymore.

The most reliable way to prevent gout is to lose weight, consume lots of vitamins, and avoid alcohol.

According to specialists, dietary supplements do not have any effect on gout, but Dr. Sebi advises us to drink burdock, dandelion, and elderberry teas. Eating alkaline fruits and vegetables also helps to lower the uric acid levels.

9.   GERD (gastroesophageal reflux disease)

GERD is a long-term condition in which stomach contents rise in the esophagus. The leading cause is inadequate closure of the esophageal sphincter, but obesity, obstructive sleep apnea, and gallstones are also involved.

We must change our lifestyle, eat healthily, start exercising, stop smoking, and most certainly let go of acidic foods. That's why Dr. Sebi's nutritional guide will give us a hand to defeat this ailment.

10.   Asthma

Asthma is a chronic inflammation of the longs, due to excess mucus accumulation, environmental and genetic causes.

It's quite hard to prevent it, but easier to cure. Traditional medicine uses vitamins, fatty acids, respiratory maneuvers, and breathing techniques to maintain the lungs' proper function.

Dr. Sebi advises us to use fennel, anise, chamomile teas, and alkaline fruits and vegetables.

Chapter 4: Cancer Treatment

Cancer cells themselves produce acid and increases the acidic content in the blood and the rest of the body. In this case, if a cancer patient continues to take foods that have a high level of acid, it implies that there is going to be a big problem associated with the health of the individual.

There are many foods mentioned and used by Dr. Sebi for the treatment of cancer. He pronounced that many herbs are very good for the prevention and cure for cancer. He claimed that many cancer patients do not need chemotherapy at all. All they need is to stick to the natural herbs that combat this illness.

Dr. Sebi recommends that foods that are rich in alkaline contents are the best for fighting cancer cells. It makes the internal body organs to remain increased in alkaline.

More so, there are significant proofs in different studies that reducing the consumption of meat and the intake of vegetables, fruits, and some numbers of grains might prevent cancer. Well, this can not only prevent cancer, but it can also cure cancer if dieters can adhere strictly to the approach of Dr. Sebi's diet.

Many bodies in the U.S that investigate cancer stated that the patient's health is most likely related to his diet in such that when he consumes vitamins (vitamin C, vitamin A, and sometimes fiber) might lessen the danger of cancer.

Also, the American Cancer Society mentioned that individual who takes in alkaline diet and avoid foods that are processed such as; high-fat foods, soft drinks, and junks. Foods that are beneficial and does the body well are a rich source of vegetables and fruits.

Dr. Sebi's Magic Approach For Prostate Cancer

Dr. Sebi technically applied close observation and regular supervision with the sufferers after the administration of appropriate therapy for prostate cancer.

He usually gave treatment to cure the ailment of the fundamental cause, after he had gotten full health history from the sufferer.

The sufferer will be subjected to Thirty days Fast phase one detoxification and cleansing to degenerate tumor growth and fortify healthy cells.

Dr. Sebi Recommended Herbal Items For Prostate and Breast Cancer

- Pavana (Croton tiglium)

- Cordoncillo negro or Matico (Piper aduncum)

- Kalawallia (Polypodium leucotomos)

- Burdock Root (Arctium lappa)

- Contribo (Aristolochia trilobata)

- Nettle Root

- Cupressus sempervirens

The herbal recipes for Cancer can be used separately through the infusion method of Dr. Sebi's herbal preparation.

Dr. Sebi Good To Do It Yourself

It is excellent to think about how to preserve your newly harvested plant after you have used enough of the cleanser to purify your body as a result, the first thing of the powdered form.

Preparation of Powdered Form

Do the preparations of the herbs separately when you have completed the processes, the preparation dosage can be determined.

- Harvest the herbs from the original source.

- Gently clean the herbs with pure water.

- Dice the herb into pieces

- Use clean Mortar and Pestle to pond it into a thin layer to expose the plant tissue to hot-air, to facilitate quick and perfect dryness.

- Spread the herbs on foiled racks or aluminum trays and sundry or use hot air oven at 180 – 200°C. Make sure you are turning the tray 90° at every 10 – 15minutes, till it dries if you are using the hot-air oven.

- Grind the dried herb with a grinder to produce powdered form.

Preparation of Dr. Sebi Dosage for Cancer

To Combine All Dr. Sebi Herbs

- Measure 1 Teaspoonful from each powder listed above for Prostate Cancer.

- Pour the powder inside a kettle and add 3 cups (750ml) of water.

- Put the Kettle on a heat source, at the boiling point leave it for 8 – 12minus to boil and allow it to cool for some minutes to warm.

- Drink at night only after a meal before you sleep.

Alternatively,

For Single Dr. Sebi's Herb

- Measure 1 Teaspoonful Cancer Powder

- Pour the powder inside a kettle and add 1 cups (250ml) of water.

- Put the Kettle on a heat source, at the boiling point leave it for 8 – 12minus to boil and allow it to cool for some minutes to warm.

- Drink at night only after a meal before you sleep.

You may also diffuse the powder in hot water.

Ready To Use Herbs

Many of the Dr. Sebi enlisted herbs for Cancer treatments are primarily available on the Amazon platform to be purchased.

Second Phase

You will need to follow all the nutritional requirements and reenergize your body system with the below herbs:

- Sarsaparilla Root

- Sea Mose (Iris moss)

- Pao Pereira

- Soursop

- Anamu also called Guinea Hen Weed.

- Sage

Dr. Sebi Herbal Remedy for Prostatitis

The prostate often occurs in man's prostate gland. The prostate gland is situated under the urinary bladder and the branched ejaculatory duct that link with Urethra pass through it. When Prostate is infected it enlarges and contracts the two ducts that passed through it, which in turn prevent the passage of urine from the bladder through Urethra with severe pain or contraction.

The natural cleansing herbs to prevent or cure prostatitis by using Dr. Sebi.

28g of Dr. Sebi's Ready to Use Herbs Produce

- 1 Teaspoonful Blessed Thistle

- 1 Teaspoonful Prodigiosa

- ½ Teaspoonful Cascara Sagrada Herb

- 1 Teaspoonful Rhubarb Root

100g of Dr. Sebi's Ready to Use Herbs Produce

- **1 Teaspoonful** Cupressus sempervirens

- 1 Teaspoonful Burdock Root (**Arctium lappa)**

Preparing Techniques to Combine All Dr. Sebi Herbs

- Measure 1 Teaspoonful from each powder listed above for Prostatitis but take ½ Teaspoonful of Cascara Sagrada Herb.

- Pour the powder inside a kettle and add 2 cups (500ml) of water.

- Put the Kettle on a heat source, at the boiling point leave it for 8 – 12minus to boil and allow it to cool for some minutes to warm.

- Drink at night only after a meal before you sleep.

Note: Confirm how many times you defecate before you increase the dosage. If you are frequently passing bowel once or twice daily, you do not need to increase the dose but if you scarcely defecate once daily you can start using the herbal medicine before a meal in the morning and after a meal at night.

Lifestyle Change and Recommendations

The way and manner we live can have severe effects on our health and wellness. This also pertains to people who have been diagnosed with cancer. A healthy lifestyle can help in treating cancer and also assist you to be well. It might even make your long-term health much better.

Healthy living simply refers to adopting positive behavior alterations as part of a life-long and continual process. To select areas for your health improvement, we suggest you focus on these six factors, which we refer to as the "Mix of Six." Each of these factors helps the other and contributes to their effectiveness.

1. Accept practical and emotional support

- If you have a network of people who are encouraging you, it is advantageous for your health, mostly emotional encouragement or support. Research conducted has put side by side individuals who had the most and smallest amount of social support. It was recorded that those people who had the most social support had a much better quality of their healthy life, and they stayed longer periods in life.

- Below are some recommended ideas for building a support system:

- Request for assistance or for someone who can listen. Individuals, in most cases, want to assist but do not know how to go about it. Therefore, you will have to be precise and state your request.

- Enter into a support group. Sharing with other people who have related experiences might assist you to cope.

2. Manage Stress

- Lowering your stress level can assist you in managing your physical and mental health. Below are some tips for managing stress:
- Make use of relaxation systems, which include meditation, yoga, and guided imagery.
- Make out short periods to meditate or think all through the day. This could mean taking time to be careful while washing your hands, chilling at a stoplight, or brushing your teeth.
- It can be of help put away 20 minutes or more each day for stress management practices.

3. Get enough sleep

- Endeavor to sleep for 7-8 hours per night. This will help improve your health, mood, weight, memory, attention, control, coping ability, and so much more.

- Set a time for sleep and endeavor to follow it. Also, set weekday and weekend sleeping time the same way.
- Endeavor to make your bedroom as dark as you can.
- The bedroom temperature should be cool.
- Stay clear of screen time before sleeping. This means the time you set aside on smartphones, backlit tables, and TV.
- Do not take stimulants such as sugar, caffeine, and alcohol.

4. Exercise regularly

Endeavor to exercise while cancer treatment is ongoing and after cancer treatment. This can assist in lessening weight gain, loss of strength, and weakness. Also, do not try to sit or stay on the bed for a long time.

Dr. Sebi Fitness tips During Cancer Care:

- Build and form a fitness routine that is not dangerous for you.
- Add an aerobic activity. This will enable your heart pump.
- Also, add strength exercise.
- Look for means to walk when you should be sitting down.
- Cut short your sitting time by standing upright each hour.
- Join in short bursts of exercise all through your day.
- Integrate physical activity into time with friends, trips, and family events.
- Endeavor to talk to your health care team about building an exercise plan; this is secure and right for you.

5. Eat well

A healthy diet can assist you to control cancer side effects, improve health, and recover speedily. It might also reduce your future chances of cancer. Below are some tips to assist you in building healthy eating habits:

- Add a collection of vegetables in each meal. The vegetables should be the major part of your meal, not an option.
- Consume foods that have high fiber. High fiber foods include beans, peas, seeds, nuts, whole grains, and lentils.
- Add prebiotic and probiotic foods to support a healthy gut. Probiotic foods are listed as sauerkraut, yogurt, kefir, or other fermented vegetables, including kombucha, kimchi, miso, pickles, and tempeh. While prebiotic foods have high fiber,they include Jerusalem artichoke, raw garlic, chicory root, dandelion greens, cooked or raw onion, raw leeks, legumes, beans, and raw jicama.
- Select lesser red meat such as lamb, goat, bison, pork, beef, and more poultry, fish, and plant-based proteins like beans.
- Do not consume processed meats like sandwich meats, sausages, bacon, salami, and hot dogs.
- Add monounsaturated fats and omega-3 in your daily diet. Good sources are listed as walnuts, canola and olive oil, olives, flaxseed, avocado, and chia seeds. Coldwater fish such as trout, salmon, tuna, and halibut, are good sources of the listed healthy fats.
- Consume lesser portion sizes. A simple way to begin is to use smaller bowls and plates when you eat.

- Study the period to know the time you feel hungry, and when you have eaten enough. In some cases, our bodies mistake hunger for thirst and otherwise. Endeavor to drink water first if you feel hungry when it is not food time yet.
- Do not take low-nutrient and high-calorie foods. These add up to fruit-flavored drinks, sweets, candy, and sodas. Select fruit or dark chocolate in lower portions as options to sweets.
- Consume less refined "white" foods. These are listed as white sugar, white rice, and white bread. These foods are produced and made in a manner that takes away minerals, fiber, and vitamins.
- Lessen the intake of alcohol. Men should endeavor not to drink more than two alcoholic drinks each day. Women should also endeavor not to drink more than one alcoholic beverage each day.

If you are taking cancer treatment, it is vital and necessary to work with a registered dietitian nutritionist specializing in oncology to build a safe eating arrangement for you.

6. Avoid environmental toxins

Reduce your exposure to environmental toxins that can raise your chances of having cancer and other deadly diseases, which include asbestos, formaldehyde, tobacco smoke, styrene (seen in Styrofoam), and tetrachloroethylene (perchloroethylene).

Chapter 5: Diabetes Treatment

Alkaline Diet Benefits for Diabetics

The supernatural occurrence of an alkaline diet will help improve the general health of the people experiencing diabetes. As it accomplishes for other individuals, the alkaline diet will help support their body physiology and digestion, just as their insusceptible framework. This diet will enable people with diabetes to have superior control of their glucose. It is likewise going to help not only in diminishing their weight gain and the dangers of cardiovascular diseases, yet in addition to keeping their cholesterol level low.

The alkaline diet permits a superior administration of diabetes and, accordingly, it assists people with diabetes with staying away from all the more effectively the degenerative diseases associated with their condition. So by following an alkaline diet, in spite of their health circumstances, people with diabetes can, simultaneously, live healthier and expand their future significantly.

Diabetics Acid-Alkaline Food Chart

As a rule, individuals who need to pursue an alkaline diet need to choose their day-by-day nourishment things from an 'Acid-Alkaline Foods Chart.' We as of late distributed a 'Diabetics Acid-Alkaline Food Chart.' The utilization of this particular outline enables people with diabetes to fit in with both the alkaline diet rule and the glycemic list rule. The alkaline diet rule sets wholesome general rules. As per this diet plan, our day-by-day nourishment admission ought to be made out of at least 80 percent of alkaline-framing nourishments, and of close to 20 percent of acidifying nourishment items. Moreover, the diet features that the more alkaline a nourishment thing is, the better it is really. Then again, the all the more acidifying a nourishment item is, the more awful it ought to be for the human body.

Concerning the glycemic file rule, it separates nourishments into four fundamental classes regarding their capacity to raise the glucose. This capacity is presently estimated by the glycemic record GI that reaches from 0 to 100. (1) Foods that contain no carbohydrates and that have, in the outcome, an unimportant glycemic list (GI~0); people with diabetes may take them uninhibitedly. (2) Foods containing carbohydrates with a low glycemic index (GI 55 or less); individuals with diabetes ought to eat these items with some precautionary measures. (3) Foods that have carbohydrates of the high glycemic file (GI at least 56); people with diabetes must, so far as could be expected under the circumstances, reject them from their diet. (4) Processed nourishments; people with diabetes should counsel the producers' names to make sense of their specific glycemic list esteems.

Diabetics Top Best and Top Worst Foods

Expected for the individuals influenced by diabetes, the 'Diabetics Acid-Alkaline Food Chart' separates nourishments into six classifications. The rundown underneath goes from the top best to the topmost noticeably awful nourishments.

1. Alkalizing nourishment things with GI~0. They are among the top best nourishments. People with diabetes may eat them uninhibitedly.

Asparagus; parsley; broccoli; carob; celery; lettuce;; vegetable juices; mushrooms; garlic/onions; squash; okra; green beans; zucchini; cauliflower; beets; cabbage; crude spinach; lemons; avocados; limes; goat cheddar; herb teas; stevia; lemon water; ginger tea; green tea; canola oil; olive oil; flax-seed oil.

2. Alkalizing nourishment items that have a GI of 55 or less. Individuals who have diabetes should take them with balance, on account of their glycemic record.

Grain grass; sweet potato; carrots; crisp corn; olives; peas/soybeans; tomatoes; bananas; fruits; pears; oranges; peaches; grapefruit; mangoes; kiwi; papayas; berries; apples; almonds; Brazil nut; wild rice; chestnuts; coconut; quinoa; hazelnuts; lentils; soy milk; soy cheddar; goat milk; bosom milk; crude nectar; whey.

3. Acidifying nourishments with a GI~0. People with diabetes ought to expend them with an alert, being their acid-creating character.

Rhubarb; cooked spinach; pork; shellfish; liver; clams; meat; venison; sheep; cold-water fish; chicken; turkey; eggs; spread; buttermilk; curds; cheddar; corn oil; fat; margarine; sunflower oil; wine; lager; espresso; cocoa; tea; mayonnaise; molasses; mustard; vinegar; fake sugars.

4. Acidifying nourishments having a GI of 55 or less. Considering both their acid-shaping element and their glycemic record, individuals with diabetes should eat them with limitations.

Lima beans; naval force beans; kidney beans; pinto beans; blueberries; cranberries; sharp fruits; prunes; plums; dark-colored rice; grew wheat bread; corn; oats/rye; entire wheat/rye bread; pasta/baked goods;

wheat; pecans; peanuts; pistachios; cashews; walnuts; sunflower seeds; sesame; yogurt; cream; crude milk; custard; homogenized milk; dessert; chocolate.

5. Alkaline-framing nourishments with a GI of at least 56. As a result of their high glycemic file, these items are among the most exceedingly awful nourishments for people with diabetes. Along these lines, individuals who experience the ill effects of diabetes need to maintain a strategic distance from them.

Turnip; beetroot; tofu; potato with skins; figs; grapes/raisins; dates; melons; pineapple; maple syrup ; watermelon; rice syrup; amaranth; raw sugar; millet.

6. Acid-creating nourishments with a GI of at least 56. These things are excessively acidic and have too high-glycemic list carbohydrates. They speak to the topmost noticeably awful nourishments for people with diabetes. In this way, people living with diabetes need to cut them totally from their dinners.

White bread; buckwheat; pumpkin; white rice; spelled; potatoes w/o skins; white sugar; dark-colored sugar; prepared nectar; soda pops.

Dr. Sebi's Nutrition That Cuts Out The Sugar

Taking out sugar might be more of a drastic way, but if there is any diabetic medical condition that requires this, then you are left with no other choice. However, you still have hope as there are still methods to cut out the sugar content of a food item without having to make the food item either boring or tasteless.

Cutting the Sugar

For your breakfast options, which include cereal, try to add dried berries, cinnamon, apricots, or other kinds of dried fruits, which will assist it in leading to a naturally sweet flavor that would be the best option for a diabetic patient. Another method that you can use to cut out the sugar content is to use strawberry or homemade raspberry sauce on pancakes and waffles rather than the sweetened syrup.

If it is possible, try to replace sugar with fruit purees as they contain natural sugar and it is also one of the best options for a diabetic patient. This is most important when there are recipes that need the inclusion of one or more cups of sugar as the measurements for the ingredients.

When you want to prepare vegetable dishes, try to add some sweeter vegetables alongside strong-flavored vegetables as it will assist in sweetness and will be beneficial to the taste of the dish.

In that case, you will have to use a combination of ginger and carrots, mashed sweet potatoes with cinnamon, spinach with nutmeg and other relevant combination which a person finds pleasing. When you buy pre-prepared food items, try to look for the food items that have the right labeling and will also permit the diabetic patient to make the right decisions and but the products that do not possess high sugar content. It is also possible to eliminate sugar if you try to cut it out little by little rather than all at once.

Dr. Sebi Herbal Supplements For Type 2 Diabetes

This is a disease that builds because of the issue associated with the hormone insulin, which is produced by the pancreas. In cases where this process is interrupted due to irregularity, there is not enough control of the glucose in the blood and the amount that is taken into the cell. However, there are a few of the medical and home remedies that can be taken a look at to control this abnormality within the body.

Natural Sugar Control

Outlined below are a few recommendations of home remedies that should be taken a look at when you want to reduce the problems of diabetic patients:

Taking Alpha lipoid acid assists in managing the sugar level in the blood, and it is seen as one of the best multipurpose antioxidants.

Taking 400mcg a day. Chromium picolinate helps insulin to keep the sugar levels in the body low. The Chromium picolinate keeps the blood sugar level when you take the right insulin.

Taking garlic is another essential method of assisting the circulation and control of sugar levels. It comes in suitable capsules for easy and stress-free consumption.

500mg of L-glutamine and taurine each day will assist in bringing down the sugar cravings and also help to release the insulin the right way. It is useful for people who have problems managing their intake of sweet food items.

Huckleberry is the best option for improving the production of insulin in the body when it is taken with the right prescription. It is a natural remedy that is recommended for consumption.

A mixture of tea and kidney beans, navy beans, white beans, lima beans, and northern beans does assist in eliminating the toxin from the pancreas.

There are more natural remedies that are used in managing blood sugar levels in diabetic patients. Meanwhile, the listed remedies should be consumed with either medical authorization or advice from some experts who have a deep understanding of the diabetic disease.

Root Vegetables And Fruits For Diabetics

Because of the several health problems that can happen in the body of a diabetic, it is necessary to be careful with the diet plan taken every day.

Fruits and Veggies

Any consumption of food needs to be done with some level of sensitivity to make sure it is the best for the diabetics. Every diabetic patient needs to make sure they follow the balanced diet which is rich in minerals and vitamins. Also, the foods which have protein, fats, and carbs should be at an acceptable level.

Root vegetables and fruits have been taken as a huge source of minerals and vitamins and fiber which is vital in reducing the chances of heart attack and stroke occurring chances. These root vegetables and fruits generally assist in making up for any side effects the distressed blood sugar level causes. These side effects are expected to lead to heart attacks and blindness if not managed effectively by the regulating ingredients of minerals and vitamins gotten from the root vegetables and fruits.

It should be taken into notice that eating root vegetables and fruits is a mixture of other food items that are seen as the best for diabetic patient consumption rather than eating them without taking in snacks. It is so because when these root vegetables are eaten together with other foods, the chemical reactions will let all the vitamins and the minerals to be easily absorbed in the body system and this will lead to a controlled blood sugar level.

However, when it is taken in as a standalone item like snacks, the blood sugar levels are likely to be increased as the absorption levels will be twisted and lower than optimum. The most vital point to take notice of is to make sure that any food you eat should be done in a mixture that lets the absorption levels to be the best for the patient with diabetics to take in.

Chapter 6: Chronic Disease (Kidney) Treatments

Basically, any problem with your kidneys might lead to your blood not being purified well. This causes toxins to be accumulated in the blood. You might have a family history of kidney problems, high blood pressure, and diabetes. Recent studies show that overusing normal medications for various diseases can play a huge role in deteriorating the health of your kidneys.

Many people are habitual users of medications, even for the slightest aches and pains. You have probably done it since you didn't know that these drugs could harm your health, including your heart, liver, and kidneys. Many people today have moved to a more holistic approach for their health. Dr. Sebi knew what some scientists are trying to prove today. He might have known that people today would need his help in curing their kidney problems. Yes, he created a herbal remedy for kidney problems.

If you have been diagnosed with kidney disease, following Dr. Sebi's diet can help you. Make sure you talk with your doctor if you feel like something isn't quite right with your health. When you think about all the toxins being put into our bodies today, it isn't any wonder that there are so many people with kidney problems.

Ingredients in the Kidney Disease Kit

Dr. Sebi's kit combines many healthy and rare herbs that he thought were perfect for kidney problems. Unfortunately, not all problems can be treated with the same herbs. Dr. Sebi's kits let you customize them for your needs. Let's look at the ingredients.

UTI Special Mix

UTIs are the most common problem with kidneys. If you are constantly getting UTIs, this might help you stop getting them.

Kidney Stone Hunter

This herbal mix works against kidney stones. Even if you don't get kidney stones, this can help detoxify your body.

AHP Zinc Powder

Ayurvedically herb purified (AHP) zinc powder can be taken by anyone who has a zinc deficiency. Zinc deficiency can cause kidney problems.

Swarna Bang Tablets

This combination of herbs has been used for thousands of years to fight recurring UTIs. These are strong enough to help the kidneys, too.

Chandanadi Tablets

This herbal combination includes Dsaruharidra-Berberis aristata, sandalwood oil, karpoora, rala-shorearobusta, amalaki, acacia catechu, kattha, gandhabirojasatva, sugandhamaricha, and sandalwood. These herbs are combined in the correct proportion to get the perfect outcome.

Punarnava Special Kidney Mix

Some reports published about kidney disease claim panarnava is one herb that helps the kidneys function properly.

Cure For Kidney Problems In Dr. Sebi's Way

Dr. Sebi, in one of his lectures, spoke extensively on how he handled kidney problems, especially acute and chronic kidney diseases.

This process should begin immediately after the fasting process has ended.

First, use iron liquid, which replenishes of the amount of minerals needed for the body.

The Dr. Sebi liquid iron plus and Bio Ferro provides an increased amount of iron for the blood purifies and remove every toxin substances in it. The Bio Ferro helps in increasing the frequency of urination to assist in toxin elimination.

Second, employ alkaline herbs, which contain an increased amount of potassium in the body. This helps in the opening of the kidney to ensure easy urination.

The Dr. Sebi potassium phosphate, known as FOCUS, is a natural diuretic that helps in flushing out excess fluid, toxins, and acids in the body. This herb contains an increasing amount of magnesium, calcium, and phosphates.

Ensure you follow the Dr. Sebi instructions written on the package and continue to take the herbs until you achieve your desired result.

Treatment And Passage Of Kidney Stones

The treatment of kidney stones requires the intake of alkaline herbs that are beneficial for consumption as food and the use of medicinal herbs. This means you have to consider both methods to be able to fight kidney abnormalities and problems.

The diet, which comprises vegetables, fruits, and grains, contains high magnesium and calcium because a reduced amount of these minerals could result in kidney stones problems.

Let us look at the herbs that are effective for the treatment and ejection of kidney stones.

Herbs Used For The Treatment And Ejection Of Kidney Stones

There are some specific herbs that are very effective for fighting kidney stone disease. Some of these herbs are very common and will help you greatly for the cure of kidney stone and its ejection.

The herbs perform there functions by relieving edema in the ureter mucosa, decreasing spasm that occurs as a result of irritation by calculus, and improving the flow of urine.

Examples of these herbs are:

- Saw palmetto fruit.

- Dandelion leaf.

- Lobelia flower, seed and leaf.

- Goldenrod leaf or flower.

- Horsetail leaf.

- Khella seed.

- Madder root.

- Gravel root.

- Horse chestnut fruit.

- Corn silk.

- Couch grass.

- Hydrangea root.

Constituents And Scientific Backup Of Kidney Stone Removal Herbs

Saw palmetto fruit

Saw palmetto fruit contains many ethyl esters of fatty acids, enzymes, tannins, resins, terpenoids, and sitosterols.

It is a reliable plant used for the treatment of sufferers with Benign Prostate Hyperplasia (BPH). The herb contains tonic that helps the urinary tract, and it is used for both male and female sufferers.

This fruit contains spasmolytic effects, making it easy for the removal of stones, and it also benefits patients with dysuria and tenesmus. This herb reduces the pressure on the bladder and has a sedative effect on an irritated detrusor, which assists sufferers with bladder and prostate abnormalities.

Dandelion leaf

This plant leaf is a very effective leaf which helps in the tonification and detoxification of the liver and kidney. The leaf is a strong diuretic, and it is compared to furosemide in animal studies. It has also been carried out in humans, and it was discovered that the effects are similar. Animal studies have shown that dandelion leaf is important in the removing of kidney stones via the direct passage.

Dandelion is one of the major sources of potassium with about 4.25% potassium compared to other drugs, which produces a lesser amount. It can be used as a diet and medication because of its ability to improve the urinary, biliary system.

Lobelia flower, seed, and leaf

Lobelia contains powerful relaxant and antispasmodic effects that assist the urinary stones to pass through the ureters easily. This plant is regarded as acetylcholine antagonists though other mechanisms may speak for its broncho and ureter-relaxing effects.

Goldenrod leaf or flower

This herb is used as strong urinary stimulants, which help in the improvement of diuresis and reduction of albuminuria in the kidney.

It is also very important for the treatment of nephritis and helps is the stabilization of the body immediately after the kidney has discharge stones. This means it should be used immediately after the kidney stone has been ejected.

The presence of flavonoids in the plant helps in the repair of the kidney, blood vessels, and connective tissues surrounding the kidney.

Horsetail leaf

Horsetail leaf is very effective for the repair of connective tissues that surrounds the kidney and the lungs due to the presence of silica component in it.

Horsetail also helps in diuresis, and it is a general metabolic stimulant that increases connective tissue resistance. It is important in both acute and chronic removal of kidney stones.

Khella seed

Khella plant, especially the seed, contains khelin and visnadin as its active components, which make it useful by acting as a mild calcium–channel blocker in the dilation of the ureters.

Visnadin contains some smooth-muscle relaxing components which is associated with the non-standard calcium-channel activity.

The active components present in khella seed is excellently absorbed and have reduced toxicity as evidenced by the almost total lack of side-effects with long-term use in the treatment of an individual with asthma.

Corn silk

Corn silk is a very important herb as it is used for increasing the easy flow of urine, and it contains a demulcent property that helps in reducing irritation from stones and facilitating its easy removal.

This plant should be collected fresh, especially when it is still very green, in order to prevent the consumption of the low-quality herb.

Madder root

Madder root is significant and used by patients with kidney problems because it has a spasmolytic effect on the ureters and enables the free passage of stones. This plant was studied, and it shows to contain calcium-channel antagonizing effects, which might contribute to relaxing smooth muscle.

This plant is also used to prevent calcium and phosphate oxalate salts from forming kidney stones in the body.

Gravel root

This plant used for the treatment of urinary gravel

Gravel root can dissolve concretions. It is used for the treatment of urethritis, cystitis, irritable bladder and fluid retention.

Horse chestnut fruit

This plant used for the treatment of various health conditions because of the presence of anti-edema properties known as escin. Escin reduces small pore number and diameter in capillary endothelium, thereby decreasing fluid seepage into the tissue spaces (Longiave D. et al, 1978).

The presence of calculi in the ureter is easily removed with the use of this plant. The plant anti-edema properties help in the production of enlargement of the internal diameter of the ureter, thereby helping the stones to migrate easily even in resistant cases.

Couch grass

This plant is a saponin and mannitol-containing diuretic that contain some silica. This herb helps in the repair of irritated mucosal walls and has been used to treat prostatic adenoma.

This plant helps in the easy removal of stones and helps in repairing and preventing recurrence of kidney stones.

Hydrangea root

This plant is important and useful for the easy removal of stones. It is also helpful for sufferers who have urinary tract infections and prostate enlargement.

Chapter 7: HIV/STD Treatment

The same strategies to prevent any other STD are the same strategies that you should use to decrease your risk of contracting HIV. There are some medications that people can take that can keep them from contracting HIV, but these are normally only given to patients who are at a higher risk of contracting it.

Dr. Sebi offers an alternative to modern medicine when it comes to treating HIV. He believes that cleaning the mucus build-up in the lymphatic system and blood can help HIV.

Dr. Sebi didn't create something specifically to treat HIV/AIDS or any specific disease. Instead, he came up with compounds that are meant to cleanse the body and provide important nutrition. However, when you want to focus on cleansing your body of major illnesses, the interest will then turn to compounds that are found in his therapeutic packages.

We are all dealing with the fatigue and cellular stress because we are constantly exhausting out oxygen supply. And we are constantly trying to find any means to remain hydrated to deal with our suffocation through animal products, medical-chemicals, starch, and sugar.

We need out mucous membrane to maintain health because it helps to protect the cells. If this mucus is broken down, it becomes pus and will then expose your cells, which is what causes disease.
Now, when we are fasting, it will cause our bodies to form more oxygen. Then we start to provide our bodies with foods that are rich in potassium phosphate and iron fluorine, which helps to flush out toxins, tumors, and mucus from our internal walls. The reason we need to cleanse ourselves is that we know that our liver, intestines, and pancreas are power players for the best circulation. This will help to treat HIV/AIDS.

The only thing that is going to cause your body to start harming your mucous membranes is acid. This erosion in the body will create a greater oxygen deprivation. It is important that when you eat, you consume natural greens and fruits. Any grains you eat should not be man-made, and that all oils you use can retain nutrition once it is processed. Springwater will also help you to maintain your mineral content.

Dr. Sebi has come up with more than 40 herbs to flush your body of inflammation as well as nourish it. While many people will travel to Usha Village in Honduras to be cured of HIV/AIDs, you don't have to travel that far. All you need to do is stick to the nutritional guide and make sure you consume only alkaline foods.

The lymphatic system, skin, and blood make up the immunological system. It is important that you adhere to a strict diet to clear these areas of mucus. If you don't, it will take a lot longer to heal. To help boost your healing, you should consume only green leafy plants such as:

- Nori

- Hijiki

- Arame

- Dulce

- Wakame

- Burdock plants

- Lams quarters

- Purslane

- Nopales

- Dandelion greens

- Lettuce

You can also eat mushrooms, spices, and peppers that are on the approved foods list. When you start to follow this diet, it is important that you make sure you drink a gallon of water every day and do some light exercise. Having a gallon jug prepared for the day, at the start of the day, is a good idea, and you can count any water used in teas. You should drink red clover tea instead of chamomile.

The first thing you need to do is to address your iron deficiency because your immune system requires plenty of it. You need to take a bottle a day of either Bio Ferro or Iron Plus for ten days. After that, you only have to take two to three spoonfuls once you begin your therapeutic package. You can also consume a cup of bromide tea at noon and in the evening each day.

After that, the initial first ten days, you should start taking a mixture of different supplements. Some people will take all of them, while others only choose a select few. There are people on Dr. Sebi's website that can help guide you as to what you need to take. The following products are the ones you should look at:

- Electra Cell – breaks down calcification and strengthens your immune system, and clears out the build-up of mucus.

- Cell Cleanser – Gets rid of mucus, acids, and toxins on the intracellular level, and will improve your bowel movements.

- CC4 – Gets rid of mucus, acids, and toxins on a deeper intracellular level and will help provide you with mineral nourishment.

- Chelation – Helps to cleanse you on an intracellular level, and improves your bowel movements. It also helps your digestive tract.

- DBT –Helps to nourish and cleanse your pancreas.

- ECAL – Removes fluid and toxins from your cells' mitochondria. It is high in carbonates, phosphates, bromides, and iodides.

- Fucus – This is a natural diuretic. It will flush out stagnant fluids, dead cells, and promotes healthy skin. It contains phosphates, calcium, magnesium, and other important minerals.

- Lino – Get rids of calcification in the body. It has a lot of important minerals, which is important for the body and helps to break up and dissolve calcification.

- Lupulo – Calms the nervous system, relieves pain, and breaks up inflammation.

If you follow Dr. Sebi's diet and start taking his supplements, you can improve HIV/AIDs. That being said, it is still a good idea to continue to go to your doctor for monitoring. It is okay to take medications that your doctor prescribes while doing this. As you will read in the nutritional guide, the important thing is to take your supplements an hour before you take medications. This allows the supplements to help your body and heal your body from any ill-effects the medications could cause.

Lastly, you may have noticed that Dr. Sebi's treatments for herpes and HIV are very similar. While there are slight differences, most treatments will follow along the same lines as these. That means if you start following the treatment for one disease, you will be helping to prevent other diseases.

Chapter 8: Lupus Treatment

Lupus is a horrible long-term autoimmune disease where your body's own immune system gets hyperactive and begins to attack healthy, normal tissue. Some symptoms can include damage, swelling, and inflammation to your lungs, heart, blood, kidneys, skin, and joints.

Because of its complex nature, some people call lupus the "disease of 1,000 faces."

There are, on average about 16,000 new cases of lupus every year in the United States. There are over one million people who are living with lupus. Lupus normally only affect women and happens between age 15 and 44.

In 2015, lupus gained attention when Selena Gomez announced she was diagnosed in her teen years and had taken treatments for it. Lupus isn't contagious, and it can't be transmitted in any way to another person. There have been some extremely rare cases where a woman with lupus gave birth to a child who developed a type of lupus. This is known as neonatal lupus.

Types of Lupus

There are several types of lupus. The main ones are neonatal, drug-induced, discoid, and systemic lupus erythematosus.

- **Neonatal**

Most of the babies who are born to mothers who have systemic lupus erythematosus are usually healthy. About one percent of all the women who have autoantibodies that are related to lupus will give birth to a child with neonatal lupus.

The mother might have no symptoms, Sjogren's syndrome, or SLE. Sjogren's syndrome is another condition that can happen with lupus. Most of the symptoms include dry mouth and dry eyes.

 If a baby is born with neonatal lupus, they might have low blood count, liver problems, or a skin rash. About ten percent have anemia. The rash will normally go away within a couple of weeks. Some infants will have a congenital heart block. This is when the heart can't regulate a rhythmic and normal pumping action. The baby might need to have a pacemaker. This could be a condition that is life-threatening.

If you have SLE and want to get pregnant, you need to talk with your doctor before and make sure they keep a close watch on you during your pregnancy.

- **Drug-induced**

About ten percent of all the people who have SLE will have symptoms show up due to a reaction to specific drugs. There are about 80 drugs that can cause this condition.

These could include some drugs that are used to treat high blood pressure and seizures. They might include some oral contraceptives, antifungals, antibiotics, and thyroid medicines.

Some drugs that are associated with this type of lupus are:

- Isoniazid: this is an antibiotic that is used in the treatment for tuberculosis
- Procainamide: this is a medicine that is used to treat heart arrhythmias.
- Hydralazine: this is a medicine that is used to treat hypertension.

This type of lupus normally goes away once you stop taking the specific medication.

- **Subacute Cutaneous Lupus Erythematosus**

This refers to lesions that appear on the skin that was exposed to the sun. These lesions won't cause any scarring.

- **Discoid Lupus Erythematosus**

With this type of lupus, the symptoms only affect the skin. Rashes will appear on the scalp, neck, and face. These areas might become scaly and thick, and scarring might happen. This rash could last from a couple of days to many years. If it does go away, it might come back.

DLE doesn't affect any internal organs, but about ten percent of all the people who have DLE will also develop SLE. It isn't clear if the people already had SLE, and it only showed up on the skin or if it progressed from DLE.

- **Systemic Lupus Erythematosus**

This is the most common type of lupus. This is a systemic condition, meaning that is can impact any part of the body. Symptoms could be anywhere from extremely mild to extremely severe.

This one is the most severe of all the types of lupus because it can affect any of the body's systems or organs. It could cause inflammation in the heart, blood, kidneys, lungs, joints, skin, or a combination of any of these.

This type of lupus normally goes through cycles. During remission times, the patient might not have any symptoms at all. When they have a flare-up, and the disease is very active, their symptoms will reappear.

Causes

We know that lupus is an autoimmune disease, but one exact cause hasn't been found.

What happens?

Lupus happens when our immune systems attack healthy body tissues. It is more than likely that lupus is the result of a combination of your environment and genetics.

If a person has an inherited predisposition, they might develop lupus if they come in contact with something in their environment that triggers lupus.

Our immune systems will protect our bodies and helps to fight off antigens like germs, bacteria, and viruses. This happens because it produces proteins that are called antibodies. The B lymphocytes or white blood cells are what produce these antibodies.

If you have an autoimmune condition like lupus, your immune system can't tell the difference between healthy tissue, antigens, or unwanted substances. Because of this, our immune system will direct the antibodies to attack the antigens and healthy tissues. This can cause tissue damage, pain, and swelling.

An antinuclear antibody is the most common type of autoantibody that develops in people who have lupus. These ANA react with the cell's nucleus. All these autoantibodies are circulated throughout the blood, but some of the cells in the body will have walls that are thin enough to allow some autoantibodies to move through them.

These autoantibodies could attack the body's DNA in the cells' nucleus. This is the reason why lupus will affect certain organs but not others.

Some possible triggers might include:

- Medications: Lupus could be triggered by some blood pressure medicines, antibiotics, and anti-seizure medicines. People who get drug-induced lupus normally get better once they stop the medicine. Symptoms rarely persist after they stop the drug.

- Infections: Getting an infection could cause a relapse or initiate lupus in certain people.

- Sunlight: Being exposed to the sun could trigger an internal response or cause skin lesions in certain people.

Why the Immune System Goes Wrong?

There are some genetic factors that play a role in the development of SLE. Some of the genes in the body can help the immune system to function properly. People who have SLE, these changes could stop their immune system from working right.

One theory relates to the death of cells. This is a natural process that happens as the body renews cells. Some scientists think that because of some genetic factors, the body doesn't completely rid itself of all the dead cells. The cells that are dead and stay in the body might release substances that make the immune system malfunction.

Dr. Sebi's Cure for Lupus

Having lupus isn't a joking matter. What makes this disease even worse is the way health care professionals work with lupus patients. Some doctors want to kill your immune system with chemotherapy or begin giving you shots of concentrated starch, which is a lot worse than alcohol. They might as well just put lupus in the same boat as AIDS. The main reason that it hasn't been considered as AIDS is that it doesn't shatter the immune system. The truth of the matter is that for people who have lupus, their immune system is so screwed up that you would be better off not having one. This is why I said it might as well be AIDS.

- **What About Lupus?**

What has Dr. Sebi taught us about lupus?

Your central nervous system has been compromised because there is a yeast infection that no one has addressed right. The cells' mucous membranes are constantly being attacked and turned into pus, and mucus contributes to the cells being deprived of oxygen. Because the cells are exposed and our bodies are stressed with the effort of just trying to function properly, our central nervous system needs some serious help.

- **Living Without a Central Nervous System**

The life of our cells and nerves that are responsible for sending signals through our bodies have been challenged and diminished as more cells get compromised, and this contributes to more mucus forming in other parts of our bodies. Our bodies are still smart enough to know that it needs to be cleansed since mucus is stopping the cells from doing their job correctly. This will soon keep your organs from doing what they are supposed to do. This causes your pain receptors to go on overload to tell you that something is wrong with the body. Your brain and body want you to quit eating specific foods, and you should know what you need to quit eating. When it seems like your organs don't want to work right, they then start acting like an enemy rather than a friend. Can you guess what your immune system is saying about all this? What do you think your immune system is going to do? It is going to start attacking everything in sight. Now your organs are being attacked. They can't fix themselves anymore, and you can't even get a good night's sleep.

- **Why Worry About the Nervous System?**

Our bodies need to be able to protect and repair the central nervous system because it helps protect our immune system. They do things at the same time as long as our bodies are producing dopamine naturally. Our bodies can instinctively and immediately protect themselves by sending out phagocyte cells to protect and defend it. It already has these cells place throughout our bodies. Phagocyte cells called neutrophils are what begin attacking your organs. This causes them to die and turn into pus or mucus. We have more of these cells in our bodies than any other kind of phagocytes. These stationary cells called macrophages will begin eating right where they are at. They are only following orders, and they don't know what is good and what is bad. Pain receptors begin going off. But they aren't finished yet. Our central nervous system has some tough guys in the blood. They are called our "natural killer cells." Just imagine what is going to happen when these get confused about who their enemy is? These cells patrol the lymphatic and blood systems, just trying to find any abnormal cells. They will kill off healthy cells faster than they can erode away.

- **You Now Have a Compromised Central Nervous System**

Your body is confused, and your immune system sets off a fever so that your metabolism gets faster trying to repair everything quickly. This fever begins attracting histamines to areas that have been damaged so they can help call the phagocytes. Now, your body feels as if it has the flu. By this time, the immune system is using the fever to help heal; it is also calling the bones to help trigger leukocytosis. This is when the bone marrow begins producing more neutrophils to help fight. Now, while all this is happening, guess who was supposed to be making sure that everything is being done correctly and that the right enemies have been found: your lymphatic system.

Your lymphatic and immune systems are one and the same. It is supposed to clean up the dirty cells and make them all clean and new. If it fails to do this, your blood pressure is going to drop, your lungs will fill with fluid, your ankles are going to start swelling, and your body just wants to give up and die. It isn't able to do its job correctly once the central nervous system has been compromised.

- **How to Handle Lupus?**

You get rid of it the same way you get rid of AIDS, cancer, and tumors. You use the Bio-mineral balance along with Intra-cellular chelation. These require you to eat an extremely strict diet. Intra-cellular chelation just means that you are going to clean your cells; every single cell that makes up your central nervous system and organs. You won't just be cleaning your organs but every single cell that makes the organ. Why do you need to do this? If you have cancer present in your body, it is telling you that you have a high level of acid in the body. This is a very high level of mitosis. Mitosis is a cell that eats the tissues and organs. This happens when there is a presence of acid. We have to nourish every part of our bodies at the same time. Disease requires us to nourish our bodies back to health. We need to give them Bio-mineral Balance. This along with the Intra-cellular chelation, will bring our bodies back to the way they were before.

So, what exactly are we going to do:

- We give our bodies electric cell nutrition

- We get rid of the mucus

- We stay away from foods that create mucus, hybrid foods, synthetic sugars, and starches

- We fast

Support and Coping

If you have been diagnosed with lupus, you are probably going to have a lot of painful feelings about your disease from extreme frustration to fear. There are challenges to living with lupus that can increase the risk of mental health problems like low self-esteem, stress, anxiety, or depression. To help you cope, you can try:

- **Connecting With Others**

You can try talking to others who have lupus. You can find people through message boards, community centers, and support groups. Other people who have lupus could give you unique support since they are facing the same frustrations and obstacles that you are facing.

- **Time for Yourself**

You can cope with the stress by taking time for yourself. Use this time to write in a journal, listen to music, meditate, or read. Find an activity that will renew and calm you.

- **Get Support**

Find support from your family and friends. Talk about your lupus with family and friends and explain how they could help you when you have flares. Lupus is a frustrating disease for loved one since they can't feel or see it, and you might not look like you are sick.

- **Educate Yourself**

Write down all the questions you have about lupus when they come to mind so you can ask your doctor during your next appointment. You can ask your nurse or doctor for reputable sources for more information. The more you know about your disease, the more confident you are going to feel about your treatments.

Chapter 9: Vitamins & Supplements

Supplements

In addition to eating the foods listed in Doctor Sebi's nutritional guide, you will also be required to buy his proprietary supplements. Bowman guaranteed they would aid in cleansing your body and nourishing your cells.

The recommended package is the all-inclusive option, consisting of all 20 of the available supplements. This is said to be the best option because it is the fastest means of cleansing and restoring the body.

Alternatively, you can opt to purchase individual supplements based on your health goals. Each has its unique benefits. For more details, let's take a look at some of the supplements and what they offer.

1. Green Food Plus – This supplement contains multiple minerals collected from herbs that are rich in chlorophyll. It promotes the healthy development of vital organs such as the brain, nervous system, heart, and the blood. You should take 4 capsules each day.

2. Viento – A cleanser and an energizer, Viento will revitalize your body and increase the oxygen levels in your brain and blood. It is rich in iron, which is used in the formation of hemoglobin in red blood cells. The supplement also works on your kidneys and the lymphatic, respiratory, and central nervous systems. You should consume 4 capsules per day.

3. Sea Moss/Seaweed – This nutritious plant is a rich source of calcium, magnesium, iron, and ninety-two other essential minerals. It also contains many vitamins and is quite versatile in how you can ingest it. Sea moss can be incorporated in baking, blended into smoothies, used as an ingredient for gravies, ice creams, and fashioned into desserts. It is well known for its healing aspects and ability to promote a balanced restoration of the mucous membrane, thus improving your overall health. The ailments it can help treat include skin conditions, respiratory diseases, and muscle and joint pains.

4. Testo – It works on your endocrine system. It promotes hormonal balance and improves your libido and virility, especially in men. Some claims suggest it helps increase blood flow to male genitalia, which enhances sexual responsiveness.

5. Tooth Powder – Just as its name suggests, it nourishes the teeth and cleanses your gums while preventing dental diseases such as tooth decay. The powder is applied to a wet toothbrush.

6. Uterine Wash and Oil – This wash restores the health of the vaginal canal.

7. Estro – This product promotes fertility and high libido in women. The dosage is 4 capsules every day.

8. Hair Follicle Fortifier – For hair growth and strengthened hair follicles, make a paste and apply it evenly on your scalp every day.

9. Banju – It handles conditions involving the nervous system such as stress, pain, and irritability. There is also a tonic version that caters to children with ADHD and ADD. Consume 2 tablespoons twice a day.

Other available supplements include:

- Bromide Plus Powder.

- Eva Salve for skin nourishment.

- Bio Ferro capsules for blood purification.

- Eyewash for cleansing the eyes.

- Iron Plus for fighting inflammation.

- Hair Food Oil for scalp and hair nourishment.

Something worth noting is that these supplements do not provide a guide on all the nutrients contained in them and in what quantities. This, therefore, makes it difficult to know if by taking them you will meet your daily nutritional requirements.

Recommended Additional Supplements

<u>Vitamin B-12</u>

Following Dr. Sebi's diet may result in a vitamin B-12 deficiency. An individual may avoid this by taking vitamins and fortified foods.

Vitamin B-12 is important for nervous and blood cell safety and for the development of DNA.

In general, the possibility of B-12 deficiency is present in people adopting vegan or vegetarian diets and in older adults. Doctors generally prescribe taking B-12 supplements to individuals who do not eat animal products.

B-12 deficiency signs include weakness, exhaustion, and tingling in the hands and feet. There is also a chance of pernicious anemia that prohibits the body from generating adequate red blood cells.

<u>Protein</u>

Protein helps the brain, skin, hair, hormones, and DNA health in your diet.

Under the existing recommendations, females over 19 years of age should consume 46 grams (g) of protein average daily, while males over the same age should eat 56g.

Many of Dr. Sebi's foods provide protein. For example, 100g of hulled hemp seeds produce 31,56g of protein, and 16,67g of protein in the same amount of walnuts. 100g of oven-roasted chicken breasts provide 16.79g of nutrients, for contrast.

Dr. Sebi's diet, therefore, excludes certain types of plant protein, such as rice, lentils, and soy. An individual will have to consume an extraordinarily large number of permissible sources of protein to satisfy everyday needs.

Research indicates that a large range of herbal foods is needed to consume adequate amino acids, which are protein building blocks. It may be tough to stick to Dr. Sebi's diet.

Omega-3 Fatty Acids

Omega-3 fatty acids are essential to cell membrane components. They support:

- Brain, heart, and eye health

- Energy

- The immune system

Dr. Sebi's diet contains omega-3 food products, such as hemp seeds and walnuts.

However, the body consumes these acids more readily from animal origins. A 2019 research reveals that, when you take the extension, a vegan diet includes few to none of two omega-3 fatty acids.

Anyone that practices Dr. Sebi's diet will benefit from an omega-3 supplement.

Conclusion

The alkaline diet is very healthy and encourages participants to eat more healthy plant foods and vegetables while restricting how you consume processed junk foods. These plants and herbs are nature's gift to man for treating several diseases and illness at a lesser cost than the pharmaceutical drugs.

Alkaline diet is considered safe because it is all about consuming whole and unprocessed foods.

However, the healthiest diet option is one that is rich in variety. It is important to go for a diet that has a range of different grains, proteins, vitamins, vegetables, fruits and minerals.

When you remove any single food type or group from a diet, it may make it difficult to be healthy. Although a very low protein alkaline diet can help you to lose weight, it may also increase the risk of having other weak muscles and bones. Ensure to get enough protein while on the alkaline diet. Once you are sure of getting enough protein from the alkaline diet, then you can ahead to begin this diet.

Dr. Sebi's alkaline diet is a popular diet made for curing illnesses that have been followed by many people. But scientific studies do not show that it results in curing any type of chronic disease. It is now seen as a method to lose weight and follow a healthy lifestyle to improve overall health.

Dr. Sebi was a self-proclaimed herbalist who coined this diet. He has a questionable background and education when it comes to healing people. The diet is very restrictive and difficult to follow, even more difficult than vegan dieting.

It can provide all the benefits that a low calorie and high fresh vegetable and fruit diet can give. The benefits are enormous, but the level of calories should wander close to the calories you burn on average, or else you will feel lethargic, and a process called cell starvation will start. However, if your main goal is to reduce weight, it can give promising results.

Trying different diets is a way to find out what type suits you. If you need fast weight loss and don't mind the restrictions, then this diet can be for you. To achieve the goals that you desire, you need to sacrifice some comforts of your life. We are used to being in bad routines because they don't require any effort. If we want to live healthily, we need to put some sort of effort and hard work into it.

The list of approved foods may not look like a lot to you, but it contains a variety of ingredients that can lead to great meals. However, if you think that you cannot handle this diet, then start the diet slowly by replacing one meal a week and then gradually improving on that.

Good luck to everyone who has decided to embark on the journey of alkaline dieting! I hope that you carefully follow the instructions of this diet to get closer to your desires and healthy life!

DR. SEBI FOOD LIST

COMPLETE NUTRITIONAL GUIDE FOR DR. SEBI DIET

Table of Contents

INTRODUCTION..3
    What Is The Alkaline Diet? 4
    The Benefits of Alkaline Diet...4
    Why The Alkaline Diet Beats Low Carb..5

CHAPTER 1: THE DR. SEBI NUTRITIONAL GUIDE................................7
    HOW TO FOLLOW THE DR SEBI DIET? 10

CHAPTER 2: UNDERSTANDING FOOD ELECTRICITY 11
    WHAT ARE ELECTRIC FOODS?..11
    SCIENCE BEHIND FOOD ELECTRICITY 13
    THE ALKALINE-ACID BALANCE 14
    HOW THE HUMAN BODY INTERACTS WITH ELECTRIC FOODS 18

CHAPTER 3: THE 10 COMMANDMENTS OF DR. SEBI....................20

CHAPTER 4: THE APPROVED ELECTRIC FOOD LIST.....................25
    The Sebian Nutritional Recommended Food Lists..................................25
    What You Should Not Eat...29

CHAPTER 5: TIPS FOR FOOD PREPARATION AND STORAGE 31
    BEFORE YOU BEGIN 34

CHAPTER 6: CLASSIFICATION OF FOODS..38
    Hybridized Foods...38
    Raw Foods..38
    Live Foods..39
    Genetically Modified Foods (GMO) 39
    Drugs..39
    Dead Foods..40
    The Importance of Dr. Sebi Nutritional Diets...40

CHAPTER 7: BEST ALKALINE FOODS 42

CONCLUSION 50

Introduction

Alkaline diets require a lifestyle that is totally opposite to low-carb, high-protein diets. The high protein diets wear and fatigue the individual later. It's for those who have a boring life and want to be weighed down. But the weight that is lost, recovers when the diet ends. This is not the case for alkaline diets. The diets can be integrated into one way of living, and the effects begin to show within days. They allow one to consume nearly 80% alkalizing food so that the alkaline levels of the body stay at 7.4. In comparison to its normal alkaline lean, a high protein diet tends to make the pH of the body acidic. When the pH of the body is acidic, certain pathogens become drawn and energy absorbed. The acid pH also allows the human body cells to degenerate rapidly. This adds to life being reduced. You should stay away from these failed diets and aim at fitness and vigor instead, and adopting alkaline diets.

Alkaline diets allow the body to retain its alkaline form. The different body functions are done seamlessly, and the body's immune system remains solid. Under these situations, you feel enthusiastic rather than drained. The weight shed like this also remains, and most notably, the body doesn't get tired. In other words, they repel pathogens rather than high-protein diets that tend to promote them. Such policies are also good for people with chronic diseases such as diabetes, obesity, migraine headaches, sinusitis, and osteoporosis. It helps fight these diseases from the source by adopting such a diet when taking medications.

Alkaline foods are mainly made up of fruit and vegetables. You will try and eat green vegetables and sweet fruit to make up 70 to 80% of your total food consumption. Enjoy lemons and melons as well. The list of foods to be eaten for pursuing alkaline diets also contains nuts, honey, and olive oil. It is necessary to avoid meat and fats. The acidifying items such as caffeine, beer, meats, and even certain vegetables such as cooked spinach should not comprise more than 20 percent of their diet. Alkaline water is also a must to boost health for everyone. At least 6 to 8 glasses of alkaline water will disinfect the body. Processed food is all acidic and also rich in compounds that gain weight and should, therefore, be prevented. Drinks such as sodas are highly acidic and should not be drunk at all. Thirty-two glasses of water are necessary to balance a glass of soda.

Alkaline diets are for all. We should avoid abusing our bodies and see a safe and lengthy life by making alkaline diets a part of our way of life.

What Is The Alkaline Diet?

The alkaline diet is a diet that relies on fresh vegetables and fruits in order to preserve optimum pH levels in the body. The idea is that the food we consume changes the pH of the body to be acidic or alkaline.

Followers of an alkaline diet claim that consuming a strongly alkaline diet has special health advantages, whereas a high-acidity diet disturbs the usual pH balance in the body. This triggers the depletion of vital minerals (such as calcium) as the body attempts to regain itself. This disparity is believed to increase disease vulnerability.

The diet was traditionally used to avoid kidney stones and urinary tract infections; nevertheless, not many scientists accept many of the alkaline diet's supposed health benefits.

The Benefits of Alkaline Diet

- It helps to protect your muscle density and bone mass of body

- It greatly lowers down the risk of facing hypertension and stroke

- Greatly helps to lower down inflammation and Chronic pain

- Helps to boost the absorption of Vitamin and minimizes Magnesium Deficiency

- It greatly helps to improve the immunity of the body and protects it from developing cancer

- It helps to lose weight

- An Alkaline diet will greatly increase the available energy of the body and keeps it energized all throughout the day

- It improves the health of gum and teeth

- It slows down the natural process of aging and keeps you looking younger and fresher for long

- It enhances your sexual power and increase the sexual drive

Why The Alkaline Diet Beats Low Carb

Some people got puzzled as two separate terms have been phrases "alkaline" and "alkalizing." In addition, food that tastes very acidic, such as citrus juice or apple cider vinegar, can, once digested and assimilated, have an alkalizing effect. Similarly, products that taste sweet rather than acidic, such as cane sugar, are also heavily acidified when consumed.

The Alkaline Diet vs. Popular Low-Carb Diets

You may be wondering how it compares with other traditional diets, particularly low-carb diets, including the Atkins diet and the South Beach diet if you have thought about attempting the alkaline diet.

The alkaline diet originally seems to be the exact opposite of the low-carb diet, but the facts are more complex. As you are still told, the low-carb diet limits the consumption of wheat, rice, potatoes, sugar, and beans, fruits, and vegetables. On the other side, when it comes to pork rinds, cheese, and other protein and fat-rich products, you should consume as much as you want.

By comparison, the alkaline diet restricts meat, and dairy intake, with all things, making the body more acidic. Another distinction is that while low-carb diets exclude fruit and vegetables, the alkaline diet strongly encourages certain items. This is because the most nutrients and calories accessible to fresh produce in any diet is important for anyone who wants to increase strength and lose weight.

Ironically, though, there is something growing in alkaline and low-carb diets. All diets allow people to eat fewer sugar and carbohydrates refined, but for various reasons. Low-carb diet fans mean that such excessive carbohydrates make people very far bloated during recent decades. In the words of nutrition expert Barry Sears, one big chunk of carbohydrates separated into various sacks and boxes is literally the main aisles of any foodstore. (There is also a lot of fat in these packages). Curiously, these refined carbohydrates are also acidifying. Since maize, rice and wheat, the most popular crops, produce acidifying compounds.

When you get to it, the main difference is that the low carb diet requires a nutrient, while the alkaline diet is scalpel hydrate food. True, some carbs are very dangerous, particularly if you eat too much. Nonetheless, something is off because anti-carb paranoia is so serious that people often exclude bananas, carrots, and celery from their diets. Such healthy diets are really useful and surely not because so many people are obese. These are also the secret to weight reduction, as these fill you without contributing a ton of calories to your regular intake.

Chapter 1: The Dr. Sebi Nutritional Guide

According to Dr Sebi, mucus and acidity are the cause of disease, and also eating certain kinds of food and abstaining from others could lead to an alkaline state that reduces the risk and effects of disease through the detoxification of the body since illness cannot exist in an alkaline environment. So, he designed this African Bio-Mineral theory for anyone who desires to improve their health in general and cure or prevent disease without depending on Western medicine. The African Bio-Mineral Therapy Program goal is not merely aimed at uncovering the symptoms, but to also examine and identify the cause of the disease, which in this case is Mucus. Where there is an accumulated mucus in the body, there is bound to a manifestation of disease there. Even though the African Bio-Mineral Therapy program was designed for the extraction of mucus from the body, it can also serve as a cleansing and nourishing agent to the whole entire bodily system. This is what makes this therapeutic program unique.

Fourteen days after initially taken, these therapeutic compound cleansing properties are still being released into the body since the herbs used have a natural origin. With this approach, there have been successful reversing of pathologies.

Strict compliance with the nutritional guidelines provided by Dr Sebi is very important when undergoing the African Bio-Mineral Therapy Program. The body will experience the best environment for maximum health to be achieved because the herbal compound is in synchronization with the outlined nutritional guidelines.

This diet focuses on natural, alkaline, plant-based food and herbs which involves the consumption of a certain amount of approved food with many supplements while staying away from hybrid, acidic foods that can damage the cell. Also, while following the diet, herbs are taken to nourish the cell, help cleanse the body and heal those participating in the program from years of horrible eating.

Dr Sebi was a vegan and at such the diet's composition is a list of;

- Vegetables which includes avocado, kale, wild arugula, and bell peppers,
- Grains including wild rice, quinoa, rye and spelt,
- Fruits which includes bananas, Seville orange, dates, and apples,
- Seeds and nuts including walnuts, raw sesame seeds and hemp and tahini butter,
- Herbal teas which include, fennel, ginger varieties, and chamomile
- Natural sweeteners which include, date sugar and agave syrup.
- Spices which includes powdered seaweed and cayenne and
- Oil including coconut, hempseed, olive, and avocado oils. Olive oil and coconut oil should not be used for cooking as advised by the diet. This diet must be followed through if one intends to experience the body healing itself.

According to Dr Sebi, there exist six categories of food which includes; Live, Raw, Dead, Hybrid, Genetically Modified Food and Drugs. Dr Sebi believes live and raw foods are for the "healing of the nation" and are considered to be "electric foods" for the cell since they are of alkaline origin and they help to heal the body from adverse effects that acidic food has produced. While genetically modified food, hybrid, and drug-food whether seedless fruits, weather-resistant crops like corn or anything with added minerals or vitamins should be avoided. Food like meat, poultry, and seafood, products containing yeast, sugar, alcohol, iodized salt, or anything fried that is acidic in nature should also be avoided because they negatively affect the body. Dr, Sebi also recommended these foods for people who want to live healthily, and they include; nuts, grains, butter, ripe fruits, non-starchy vegetables, quinoa, leafy greens and rye.

For the individual that enjoys eating acidic food, following raw diet mostly can seem unappetizing, you get used to it since your goal is to flush your cells of toxins which leads to the cure of disease.

How to Follow the Dr Sebi Diet?

There must be strict compliance with the rules of this diet as enumerated. The focus of these rules is to take a lot of supplements and abstaining from ultra-processed food and animal products.

Rule 1: Only food listed in Dr Sebi's nutritional guide should be consumed.

Rule 2: Every day, a gallon (3.8 liters) of natural spring water should be taken. This helps to produce the most beneficial results for the African Bio-Mineral Therapy Program.

Rule 3: Dr Sebi's supplements should be taken one hour before medications.

Rule 4: Animal products, hybrid foods should be avoided.

Rule 5: Alcohol is not allowed.

Rule 6: Only the "natural-growing seeds" mentioned in the guideline should be consumed. Avoid wheat products.

Rule 7: Avoid the killing of your food by not using a microwave.

Rule 8: Avoid canned and seedless fruits.

In addition to the above, an individual undergoing the program is expected to purchase the Dr, Sebi's cell food products which contains supplements that promise to nourish the cell and cleans the body. The "all-inclusive" package is recommended since it contains 20 different products that at the fastest rate possible claims to cleans and restore the entire body.

Also, protein is a much-needed nutrient for healthy skin, muscle and joint. Dr Sebi's diet is lacking in protein as it goes against eating beans, animal product, lentils, and soy products. One can go for any nutrient guideline since there was no specific one listed.

No specific supplement recommendations are provided besides this, and you are expected to order any supplement as par your health concerns. For instance, the capsule "Bio Ferro" claims to cleanse the blood, boost immunity, treat liver issues, aid digestive issues, increase overall wellness and promote weight loss. Since the supplements don't contain a complete list of nutrients or their quantities, it becomes difficult to determine if they will meet your needs on a daily basis or not.

Chapter 2: Understanding Food Electricity

Nutrition is a relatively new science and the concept of electric foods is even more recent. The idea behind this philosophy is that about 90% of what we eat is more or less "dead" and unsuitable for consumption. The modern diet is based on foods that are hybridized (ie most of the staple foods and many fruits and vegetables used today), fortified, genetically modified, heavily processed, or highly toxic (due to pesticides, herbicides, growth hormones, or antibiotics). Is it then surprising that our immunity, overall health, and reproductive health have deteriorated so much that we are plagued with more and more diseases that are difficult to diagnose and even more difficult to cure.

As most of these negative side effects of modern lifestyle and extensive food production have been introduced gradually, over the last hundred years, most people managed to adapt to them - some more than others. However, as the presence of processed foods, GMOs, environmental pollution, and stress have dramatically intensified over the last thirty years, what we are witnessing is a physical and mental decline of the human population on a global scale. Fortunately, these anomalies of modern society could easily be avoided or corrected with a diet change.

And this is where Dr. Sebi philosophy comes in. Dr. Sebi passionately believed that to avoid disease or heal yourself naturally if you are already sick, all you have to do is follow an alkaline diet. But, not just any alkaline diet (there are a few), but a diet based on Dr. Sebi Alkaline Food list. What sets Dr. Sebi alkaline diet apart is that it does not contain any hybridized or GM foods and includes a lot of medicinal herbs and herbal supplements. According to Dr. Sebi, in an alkaline environment, a disease cannot develop let alone thrive and spread.

So, staying healthy is about alkalizing your body. Electric foods can help you do that.

What are Electric Foods?

Electric food is food that is natural and live, which is just what your body needs to feel alive. Unfortunately, about 80% of foods in a typical Western diet are not electric. On top of that, over 90% of those foods are hybrids that are usually highly acidic and that prevent the absorption of nutrients on a cellular level. Obesity is a growing problem especially in the developed world, mainly because, despite all the food you eat, if it lacks nutrients, your body will starve on a cellular level. And when you are starving, you will want to eat but as the food you eat is usually just empty calories and your body is not really nourished, it will continue to be hungry, and you will continue to eat, and so the vicious circle continues.

Generally speaking, a modern diet is very low in nutrients. Even if you are one of those people who read the labels to check that the food you buy contains sufficient nutrition, what you probably don't realize is that those are synthetic nutrients that have been added to already dead food. Such food, being dead, cannot be properly absorbed and processed by the body.

So, it's not enough to take a certain amount of nutrients. The nutrients have to be taken in a form that your body can process and absorb. Which is not what a modern diet can do for you. On the contrary, it was created (intentionally or out of ignorance) to set us up for disease, low immunity, and addiction to antibiotics, sedatives, or sleeping pills.

Fortunately, you can avoid this trap by adopting an electric diet. How do you start?

– **Adopt an electric lifestyle**

Electric foods should become a part of your every meal every day for the rest of your life. So, this is more than just a diet. To maintain health or recover from a disease with the help of electric foods, approach an electric diet as a lifestyle.

– **Education**

Learn which foods you need to avoid and which to introduce or eat more of. If you've lived on a very acidic diet so far, you will have to introduce these changes gradually.

– **Cleanse**

To give yourself a new lease on life (which you will, with this diet) start by cleansing your body from the accumulated toxins, mucus, and fat. After the cleanse revitalize your body with Dr. Sebi revitalizing herbs.

– **Commitment**

Commit to rid yourself of unhealthy habits and addictions

As part of your new lifestyle, you will need to download a list of alkaline foods from the Internet. Don't be surprised if you come across different lists. Although all fruits and vegetables are alkaline, their pH levels vary. For a start, avoid acidic foods but during the transition period, you may eat some foods that are moderately acidic (eg dairy is acidic but yogurt is much less acidic than milk or cheese). You may find that an alkaline diet is more expensive than an ordinary diet (based on processed foods), so work out how to live on a vegan diet on a budget.

Also, print out a list of common hybrid foods and take it with you when you go shopping. Some of them are easy to recognize:

–   They lack seeds (eg seedless grapes, watermelon, apples, grapes, tangerines, etc).

–   They may have an unusual color (eg yellow watermelon, yellow cherry tomatoes, black tomatoes, etc).

–   Their name is an obvious combination of two plants, eg kalettes (Brussel sprouts and kale), peacotum (peach, apricot, and plum), etc.

3 main reasons you should avoid hybrids whenever you can:

1. They are high in sugar and starch. This sugar cannot be absorbed or used by the pancreas and liver.

2. Most of them don't have a proper mineral balance which, over time, may lead to nutrient imbalance.

3. Some hybrid foods can make Candida worse.

The common hybrid foods include carrots, corn, beets, celery, potatoes, cauliflower, rice, cashews, oats, soy, wheat, legumes, echinacea, garlic, ginseng, chamomile, etc.

Science Behind Food Electricity

Dr. Sebi referred to live and raw foods as electric foods. However, it wasn't only Dr. Sebi's view. Although the health benefits of vegan and raw diets were for a long time disapproved by mainstream science, things have, fortunately, changed.

However, not all vegan diets are created equal. They need to be carefully planned so you continue to get sufficient essential acids, vitamin B12, and essential minerals. It's absolutely crucial to stay away from most ready-made vegan meals as they are simply a vegan version of processed foods.

6 science-based health benefits of a vegan and a raw food diet:

1. **It's loaded with nutrients**

Vegan diets are based on fruits and vegetables and raw food diets are based on raw fruit and vegetables. Both these diets are high in fiber, vitamins, minerals, and antioxidants. They are also a significant source of potassium, magnesium, folate, and vitamins A, C, and E.

2. **It helps with weight management**

Vegans are rarely overweight and if they eat natural vegan foods, they simply cannot be. Many people adopt a vegan diet in an attempt to lose weight naturally.

3. **It lowers blood sugar levels and improves kidney function**

A vegan diet is a natural remedy for high blood sugar levels. Besides, diabetics who substitute meat for plant protein can easily reduce the risk of kidney disease.

4. **Protects against some types of cancer**

Studies suggest that eating fresh fruit and vegetables every day significantly lowers your risk of cancer. Besides, just avoiding animal products, even if you don't eat a lot of fruit and veg, is enough to reduce the risk of prostate, breast, and colon cancers.

5. **Lowers the risk of heart disease**

Vegans rarely have high blood pressure and one of the ways of reducing yours is to adopt a vegan diet. A vegan diet will quickly reduce both blood sugar and bad cholesterol levels.

6. **Reduces arthritic pains**

Numerous reports suggest that people struggling with arthritis would greatly benefit from a vegan diet. Consistent use of fruits and vegetables, especially raw ones, can successfully reduce pain, joint swelling, and morning stiffness, as well as provide more energy and a better mood (due to the absence of pain).

The Alkaline-Acid Balance

The key principle of two ancient medical systems, Ayurveda and Traditional Chinese Medicine is that health, happiness, and prosperity in life are all based on balance – in a diet, behavior, emotions, etc.

Although this has for a long time not been taken seriously, mainstream medicine has finally accepted that balance really IS the key to optimal health – physical, mental, and emotional.

When it comes to a diet, it's important to learn how to maintain a balance between acidic and alkaline foods. Although having alkaline blood is better than having acidic blood, if your body becomes too alkaline, you also have a problem. Besides, all your organs and systems are interconnected. So, if you improve one organ or system, functions of other organs related to it will also be improved, eg improving cardiovascular health improves the digestive system, the improved nervous system will improve the lymphatic system, etc. And when you improve the overall acid/alkaline balance of the body, you automatically improve the function of all your organs and systems.

So, to maintain health or address a particular health condition, start by improving the pH balance of your blood. This will result in a reduced risk of inflammation, improved bone health, higher energy levels, etc.

However, maintaining healthy blood pH can be tricky. Various organs have different pH and we know that blood pH should range between 7.25 – 7.45. If the pH falls below or rises above this range, you have a problem. Your blood uses a lot of energy to maintain healthy pH levels. This means that if your diet is unhealthy, ie acidic, your body will have to draw the energy it needs not from the foods you eat but from your own reserves. If this goes on for a long time, it may lead to nutrient deficiencies and many health problems.

However, if your pH levels are balanced, your health problems (if you have them) will be resolved naturally because the body is strong enough to heal and repair itself. Besides, a healthy body comes with healthy cells and a strong immune system which is the best protection against infections and chronic conditions, such as cancer or diabetes.

The best and easiest way to maintain a healthy pH level is by adopting an alkaline diet and avoiding stress (because people often eat foods high in sugar when they are trying to distress).

However, eating alkaline foods is not enough. The foods should also be organic because ALL pesticides are very acidic. This is particularly important if you have adopted an alkaline diet to address a particular health problem. Unfortunately, getting organic food is neither easy nor cheap, especially if you have a family to feed. So, if you can't grow your own food, and find buying such foods from specialized shops too expensive, try to buy directly from small farmers who are less likely to use harmful chemicals used for commercial production.

The best source of alkaline foods are fruits and vegetables, however, they come with different pH, ie some are more alkaline than others. Still, you can use this list as a rough guide to foods that will improve your alkaline/acid balance:

– **Fruits**

Apples, avocados, apricots, bananas, cantaloupes, berries, cherries, dates, currants, figs, grapefruits, grapes, guavas, limes, lemons, mangoes, nectarines, melons, oranges, passion fruits, papayas, peaches, persimmons, pineapples, pears, tangerines, raisins.

– **Vegetables**

Bamboo shoots, lima beans, green beans, string beans, beets, sprouts, broccoli, celery, cabbage, cauliflower, chicory, chard, chives, cucumber, collard greens, dandelion greens, dulse, dill, eggplant, escarole, endive, kale, leeks, garlic, legumes, okra, lettuce, onions, parsnip, parsley, sweet potato/yam, white potatoes, bell peppers, pumpkin, rutabaga, radish, watercress, turnips.

– **Nuts**

Almonds, walnuts, coconuts

– **Miscel food**

Ginger, alfalfa, kelp, clover, sage, mint, green tea, flaxseed, quinoa, pumpkin seeds, all sea veggies

– **Dairy**

Vegans don't take dairy but during the transition period, you may take some from time to time as you will probably crave many of the acidic foods you're used to. Although yogurt and kefir are dairy products they are less acidic than milk or cheese.

If you are familiar with Dr. Sebi Alkaline Food list, you will notice that many of these foods are missing from Dr. Sebi food list. The reason is that Dr. Sebi excluded all hybridized foods, even if they were alkaline and nutritious, eg potatoes, mint, garlic, parsley, beans, etc.

Acidifying foods, those that you should stay away from, include meat, dairy, sugar, grains, alcohol, coffee, chocolate, sweets, soda, and processed foods.

To find out your body's pH you can test your urine or saliva. If your urine is too acidic, try adding more veggies to your diet, eg salads, smoothies, soups, etc. If your saliva is too acidic, you probably have a digestion problem. Take digestive enzymes for a couple of days and increase your consumption of greens, eg smoothies, raw salads, steamed veggies, etc.

But what if your urine is too alkaline? This may be the result of some of the supplements you may be taking. High levels of cod liver oil, vitamin D, or magnesium and/or calcium supplements can make your urine too alkaline. Stop taking the supplements for a few days and do the test again. If your urine is still too alkaline, there's probably a digestion issue. Reduce consumption of grains, legumes, and nuts as well as meat and dairy (if you're still taking them). Re-test. Keep on experimenting until your urine tests OK. If your bowels are not working properly, take digestive enzymes for a few days.

Also, in the case of your saliva being too alkaline you need to improve your digestion so you may start taking digestive enzymes. Alternatively, to make your saliva less alkaline, you may take some vitamin C or even some acidic foods. Experiment and keep on re-testing.

Everything you eat or drink is either alkaline or acidic (or somewhere in between) and will be released into your blood. If your diet revolves around acidic foods (as most modern diets do) your body is probably overly acidic. Over the years, your bones will become weak, joints and muscles painful, and you will be at a higher risk of developing heart disease, diabetes, kidney disease, and other life-threatening conditions. This shows that longevity is directly linked to the acid-alkaline balance of your body.

Unfortunately, there is another side to the coin when it comes to eating a plant-based diet. Most people assume that just by being a vegan or vegetarian, you automatically become healthy. This is a very simplified approach to nutrition.

Ingredients that go into a plant-based diet do not have to be healthier than the ingredients of an omnivorous diet. Many of the plant-based foods are not only hybridized but are also genetically modified, eg 98% of soy. Which makes you wonder how healthy the tofu you eat really is.

Besides, we know that commercially produced fruits and vegetables are heavily treated with pesticides and herbicides. Some fruits are treated once a week for 3-4 months, ie from the moment they flower, until they are picked, eg apples, peaches, etc. That's how you get those perfect-looking fruits.

The trouble is that foods that are not natural, cannot be absorbed properly so basically eating them is a waste of time and money. Which explains why Dr. Sebi was so passionate about natural foods whose DNA had not been tampered with.

On top of that, an acidic diet is made even unhealthier by sugar-added foods, alcohol, caffeine, etc. So, the problem is not with any particular food, but with the cumulative effect of a long-term highly acidic diet and lifestyle.

However, even if you just can't give up an unhealthy diet, you can at least try to slightly improve your eating habits.

5 tips on diet improvement:

1. Have some raw leafy vegetables every day, eg as a salad, smoothie, or a snack

2. Have some fruit every day, eg as a snack between meals, as a smoothie, or as a fruit salad instead of a dessert.

3. Have green vegetables (cooked or raw) as often as you can, eg broccoli, kale, Brussel sprouts, peppers, etc.

4. Snack on nuts and seeds

5. Have avocado and berries a couple of times a week if you can

How the Human Body Interacts with Electric Foods

Your body starts changing from the moment you adopt a vegan and/or raw food diet. The first thing you will notice when you stop taking acidic foods and replace them with electric foods is higher energy levels. The nutrient level of your blood will increase and all your organs and systems will benefit from this change. After a couple of weeks, you will notice major changes in your digestion. You will either have more regular bowel movements or you will experience bloating and flatulence. This is particularly common in those who are not used to fiber-rich foods.

This problem usually resolves itself in a week or so although sometimes, especially if the transition to a new diet was sudden, it may lead to certain digestion problems. On the upside, fiber-rich foods will increase the diversity of bacteria in your gut, which is great because this strengthens your gut and boosts your immune system. On the downside, you may develop an Irritable Bowel Syndrome.

However, how your body reacts to a vegan diet depends partly on whether you're eating processed and refined vegan foods or you're following a whole vegan diet.

After several months on an electric diet, you may experience significant skin improvements and your acne may disappear. However, by now your stores of vitamin D, which you probably got from meat, fish, and dairy, may start dropping. Vitamin D is essential for healthy bones, teeth, and muscles and deficiency is linked with cancer, heart disease, migraines, and depression. The problem is that vitamin D stores last only for about two months. Unless you have regular exposure to sunlight, start eating fortified foods or take supplements.

So, a vegan diet needs to be planned and implemented carefully. If you do, after a few months, your cardiovascular health will improve and this will lower your risk of heart disease, stroke, or diabetes.

However, there is also a paradox, in that the nutrients like iron, zinc, and calcium are reduced on a vegan diet, so the body starts "stealing" them from the intestines. You may consider taking supplements, especially if you don't have time to plan and prepare healthy vegan meals.

After about 6 months on a vegan/raw food diet, your vitamin B12 stores will probably become depleted. This vitamin is essential for healthy blood and nerve cells and can only be found in animal products. Symptoms of B12 deficiency include exhaustion, breathlessness, tingling in the feet or hands poor memory. This can be prevented by taking a supplement. This is very vital because any deficiency will negate the benefits of a vegan diet for heart disease and stroke risk and can cause permanent nerve and brain damage.

There is also your bone health to take into consideration. Minerals from the foods we eat are stored in our bones and up to the age of 30, we can add minerals to this store by eating a nutrient-rich diet. However, after the age of 30, our bones become less and less capable of absorbing these minerals so eating calcium-rich foods becomes very important.

Unless you do, your body will have no other option but to draw the calcium from your skeleton to use for your other organs, which may make your bones very brittle and prone to fractures.

Unfortunately, most vegans have brittle bones and are much more prone to fractures, compared to those on omnivorous diets. Plants high in calcium are kale and broccoli but, unfortunately, plant-based calcium is difficult to absorb so it's best to take supplements.

So, although a vegan diet comes with many health benefits, you will only benefit from this way of eating if, by careful planning, you avoid nutrient deficiency

Chapter 3: The 10 Commandments of Dr. Sebi

As you may have noticed, the Dr. Sebi diet is not like any other. Where other diets either have a bunch of information that you can't figure out what it means, Dr. Sebi's diet is very straightforward. You have the food list that you have to stick with, you have the supplements that you should take, and then you have the rules we are going to go over. While the diet does require giving up a lot of stuff, it is very easy to see what you should and should not do, which, in the long run, makes it easier to follow. Let's take a look at the rules.

1.   You are only allowed to eat the foods that are listed on the nutritional guide.

The nutritional guide is the only guide you have for this diet, and those foods are the only approved foods. It really can't get any more straightforward than that. The only things that aren't really listed on the nutritional guide that you do get to consume are herbs that are most often used in supplements. Any herb that is used in Dr. Sebi's supplements, you can use in other ways as well, such as sea moss, burdock, and bladder wrack. You won't find those things on the nutritional guide, but they can be consumed in various ways and not just through the supplements.

2.   You have to consume a gallon of water each day.

That may sound like a lot, but with some planning, you can do it. Just so you know, a gallon of water comes out to 3.8 liters. Your body is made up of mostly water and it needs water to work properly. There are so many people walking around who are dehydrated and dehydration has the power to make you feel awful. Dehydration can cause you to faint, feel fatigued or irritable, look tired, breathe quickly, have a rapid heartbeat, feel dizzy, have dry skin, and so much more. While some of these only happen in severe cases of dehydration, like fainting, the other symptoms are so common that people don't even think anything about it.

For decades now we have been told that we need to drink at least eight, eight-ounce glasses of water each day. That's good advice, and it's a good place to start, but that only half a gallon. We need to push and get up to a complete gallon. A good way to get to a gallon of water is to take a gallon container and mark it at every eight ounces. You might be able to find one that already has lines on it marking each cup. Then, write times during the day where you should have consumed the water up to that point. While you don't have to be perfect about drinking water like this, it will help to keep you accountable and it will make it easier to know exactly how much water you have consumed.

3.   If you are on medications, take your Dr. Sebi supplements an hour before you take your medications.

Dr. Sebi does not want you to stop taking medications if you are currently using them. They do serve a purpose in your body, for now. Once you have followed his diet for a while and gotten rid of the disease, you can stop taking your medications under the supervision of your doctor. This will make sure that you don't end up hurting yourself more. That said, if you are currently on medication for diabetes, high blood pressure, or what have you, you need to make sure that all of your Dr. Sebi supplements are taken an hour before you take those prescriptions.

If you take your supplements and prescriptions too close together, neither is going to work correctly for you. By taking your Dr. Sebi supplements first, you are giving them a chance to protect your body and cleanse your cells. This also protects your body from the chemicals in your prescriptions. I would like to reiterate, if you are currently on prescription medication, you should not stop taking them as soon as you start the Dr. Sebi diet. Continue to take them until it is safe to stop them.

4.   You are not allowed to consume any type of animal products.

The Dr. Sebi diet is very much a vegan alkaline diet. Our body does not have to have animal products to function. First off, we are the only mammals who feed their young milk from other mammals. Cows do not ask a goat for their milk to feed their babies. Then there is the act of eating meat. If you look at any carnivorous animals out there, such as lions, bears, or wolves, they all have sharp pointy canines and claws. Humans have small canine teeth and soft fingernails. Carnivores are provided the tools they need in order to tear flesh without the need for forks and knives. Their jaws also only move up and down, which gives them the ability to tear chunks of meat out of the prey. Humans can also move their jaw from side to side and we have flat molars, which are something carnivores do not have, and they allow us to grind up veggies and fruit just like herbivores.

The digestive system also doesn't like meat. The intestinal tracts in carnivores are short, which lets meat pass quickly through them. The intestinal tracts in humans are a lot longer, like those of herbivores. This provides the body with a chance to break down fiber and to absorb nutrients from our food. True carnivores simply eat their meat raw and they rely on the acids in their stomach to break it down and kill off the bad bacteria that would, if humans did the same, kill or sicken us. The acid in our stomach is a lot weaker and this is why we rely on cooking meats, and if they aren't done properly, we wind up with food poisoning.

Wild, carnivorous animals do not develop heart disease, yet red meat is one of the top causes of heart disease in humans. Besides that, humans tend to consume too much protein in their diet, which results in insufficient fiber consumption or nutritional deficiencies. Consuming too much protein can also up your risk of heart disease and it can harm kidney functioning. Besides all of these reasons, animal products are also very acidic.

5.   You cannot consume alcohol.

Alcohol, as we all know, is very detrimental to our health, especially our liver. Alcohol is also very acidic. The liver has the hard job of breaking down harmful chemicals, and alcohol is only made up of harmful chemicals. When the liver has to work overtime in getting rid of alcohol, it can lead to cirrhosis, jaundice, and hepatitis. Alcohol is a waste product that the body wants to get, and the smallest amount affects the body. If you consume more alcohol than the body can process, you start to become intoxicated as it builds up. This will slow down how your body functions, including the immune system. This is why heavy drinkers are more likely to develop illnesses and it also increases their risk of several different types of cancer.

Alcohol use can also prevent new bone production, which places you at a higher risk of fractures and osteoporosis. It can also affect the reproductive system. Heavy alcohol use in men can cause erectile dysfunction and infertility. For women, it can cause infertility and ceasing of menstruation. A single instance of heavy drinking can have an adverse effect on the circulatory system as well.

6.   Stay away from wheat products and only eat the "natural-growing grains" that are found on the nutritional guide.

Wheat is everywhere, but wheat is not good for the body. Obviously, people with celiac disease can't process the gluten found in wheat, but wheat can also increase your risk for digestive problems, heart disease, and obesity even if you don't have a gluten allergy. Wheat aggravates the intestines, inhibits your absorptions of minerals, creates immunoreactive problems, and raises blood sugar levels. This seems to be a new phenomenon as well and that's because the wheat of today is not the same as the wheat from 50 years ago.

In the 1950s, scientists started to crossbreed wheat in order to make it heartier, better-growing, and shorter. This process introduced compounds to wheat that the human body really doesn't like. Today's wheat is hybrid and contains sodium azide, which is a toxin. During manufacturing, it also goes through a gamma irradiation process. When it comes to gluten, even for those without celiac disease, is hard for the digestive system to break it down because our body does not contain the required enzyme.

7.   Do not use the microwave to cook your food because it will kill it.

Microwave ovens were made for convenience, and convenient they are, but they aren't really good for you or your food. Microwaves turn electricity into electromagnetic waves, which are called microwaves. This makes the molecules in your food vibrate and spin, which is what makes them hot. If you rub your hands together really fast, you will be doing, basically, the same thing. The microwave does produce a type of radiation, but there are a lot of protective factors on the microwave itself that keeps the radiation from reaching you, as long as the microwave is still in good condition.

That being said, microwaving does harm the nutrients in your food. While you cannot eat garlic or broccoli in the Dr. Sebi diet, there are studies that found microwaving those foods destroys their nutrient content. For example, microwaving broccoli destroyed 97% of flavonoid antioxidants.

8.   You cannot consume seedless or canned fruits.

If you look up a definition of fruit, you would get something like "the sweet and fleshy product of a tree or other plant that contains seed and can be eaten as food." By that definition, for a food to be considered a fruit, it has to contain seeds. That means seedless fruits aren't even fruits. Why is it normal to eat fruits that don't contain seeds? You've likely had both the seeded and seedless varieties of foods and probably can't even notice a difference. But seedless fruits are not okay. They aren't even able to reproduce. The process that fruits go through to make them seedless creates something that our bodies don't even recognize, so they aren't able to use them.

Canned fruits are another best. By canned fruits, I mean those in the metal cans at the grocery store and not foods that you can naturally at home. The canned fruits at the store often contain trace amounts of BPA, bisphenol-A. The leading cause of BPA exposure is through eating canned foods. BPA exposure can lead to male sexual dysfunction, type 2 diabetes, and heart disease.

9.   You should not consume foods that are hybrid.

Hybrid and crossbreeding foods is the act of making a new plant by combining two or more species. The new species will have characteristics of their parents but is also their own unique food. This was started as a way to create plants that could be controlled or cultivated. The new species is able to live in places and conditions that its parents couldn't. This is how our modern wheat was created. By changing up the genetic order of a plant it causes the starch content to increase, which tends to be very corrosive to human tissue. Changing the genetic order of foods causes chemical and genetic mineral imbalances.

The modern corn crop is hybridized and removes all of the minerals from the soil so that nothing else will grow there. This is what caused the mid-west dust bowl. Corn also contains carbonic acid. While this may not always be the case, one way to find out if a food is hybrid is to check and see if it has seeds. A lot of our modern diseases only came about after our foods were played with. Even foods that have an organic label on them may still be genetically altered because their basic structure changed a long time ago.

Hybrid foods will not grow in nature. They are simply a product of man and have to be constantly protected and nurtured by humans. Hybrid foods have been removed from their natural content and cannot assimilate in the body and will only cause you to store toxins.

10. You cannot consume coffee or sodas, only spring water and herbal teas.

Coffee, while not innately bad for your body, is also not all that great for you either. The caffeine in coffee is addictive, which causes people to crave more caffeine. The more you drink, the higher your tolerance for it grows and the more you need to get the high you are looking for. Somebody also find that coffee hurts their stomach and digestive tract, and can also lead to heartburn and stomach ulcers. While it can be hard to give up coffee, it will be worth it in the long run because you will be allowing you natural energy to return without the need of the caffeine.

While coffee may have some redeeming properties, soda has none. Not even diet soda. This shouldn't come as a surprise to anybody, but soda is bad for you. They are jam packed full of sugar. All of this sugar does nothing for your body and will not help satiate hunger. What they do is lead to weight gain. All of this sugar will then be turn into fat in your liver. Table sugar and corn syrup contain glucose and fructose. Every cell in your body can metabolize the glucose, but fructose is only able to be metabolized in the liver. Sugary sodas are the easiest way to consume too much fructose. When you constantly drink sodas, the liver will become overloaded and will turn the fructose into fat. This can lead to nonalcoholic fatty liver disease.

Sodas are also the number one cause of type 2 diabetes. In one study performed across 175 countries, looked at the connection between diabetes and sugar consumption, found that a single can of soda increased a person's diabetes risk by 1.1%. There are also no nutrients whatsoever in soda, only sugar. It does not provide your body with anything that it can use. They also contain caffeine, which means that they are addictive. Add in the sugar, it becomes even more addictive than coffee. Sugar can cause dopamine release, which makes you feel happy. Thus, your brain equates soda to being happy.

Lastly, sodas are absolutely horrible for your dental health. The carbonic acid and phosphoric acid in the sodas create an acidic environment in your mouth, which causes your teeth to decay. While these acids are bad for your teeth, the sugar is more harmful. The sugar gives energy to the bad bacteria in your mouth. Not only is the acid eroding away at your enamel, but the bad bacteria are thriving, and this all writes disaster for your dental health.

Chapter 4: The Approved Electric Food List

The Sebian Nutritional Recommended Food Lists

Alkaline Grains List

- Fonio.

- Tef.

- Spelt.

- Kamut.

- Amaranth.

- Wild Rice.

- Quinoa.

- Rye.

Fruit List

- Peaches.

- Plums.

- Soursops.

- Dates.

- Prunes.

- Bananas.

- Cantaloupe.

- Figs.

- Prickly Pear.

- Raisins.

- Papayas.

- Cherries.

- Grapes.

- Apples.

- Mango.

- Soft Jelly Coconuts.

- Pears.

- Berries.

- Melons.

- Currants.

- Orange.

- Limes.

Spices and Seasonings

- Achiote.

- Habanero.

- Savory.

- Oregano.

- Basil.

- Thyme.

- Pure Sea Salt.

- Powdered Granulated Seaweed.

- Sage.

- Tarragon.

- Cloves.

- Dill.
- Bay Leaf.
- Cayenne.
- Sweet Basil.
- Onion Powder.

Herbs list

- Cayenne.
- Dill.
- Oregano.
- Basil.
- Onion powder.
- Pure sea salt.
- Vegetable List
- Bell Pepper.
- Chayote.
- Cucumber.
- Wild Arugula.
- Avocado.
- Green Amaranth.
- Dandelion Greens.
- Turnip Greens.
- Wakame
- Onions.

- Arame.

- Cherry and Plum Tomato.

- Dulse.

- Garbanzo Beans.

- Izote flower and leaf.

- Olives.

- Purslane Verdolaga.

- Squash.

- Okra.

- Tomatillo.

- Kale.

- Mushrooms except for Shitake.

- Hijiki.

- Nopales.

- Nori.

- Zucchini.

- Watercress.

- Lettuce except for iceberg.

Herbal Tea Lists

- Ginger.

- Fennel.

- Tila.

- Chamomile.

- Elderberry.

- Burdock.

- Red Raspberry.

Alkaline Sugar Lists

- 100% Pure Agave Syrup from cactus.

- Dried Date Sugar.

What You Should Not Eat

Foods that are not listed in the nutritional guide are not allowed to be consumed. Some examples of such foods are given below:

- Any canned product, be it fruits or vegetables, listed in the nutritional guide.

- Seedless fruits like grapes

- Eggs are not permitted.

- Any dairy product is not allowed.

- Fish is not permitted.

- Any poultry is not to be eaten.

- Red meat is strictly banned.

- Soy products, which are a replacement for meat, are also banned.

- Processed foods are not allowed.

- Restaurant foods and delivered foods are not to be consumed.

- Hybrid and fortified foods are not permitted.

- Wheat is not permitted.

- White sugar is strictly banned.

- Alcohol is banned.

- Yeast and its products are not allowed.

- Baking powder is not permitted.

Some other foods and ingredients have been cut off. You only need to follow the nutritional guide to know what you have to eat.

Chapter 5: Tips for Food Preparation and Storage

We've discussed the Dr. Sebi foods that you should make sure you have in your diet, so now we will look at the five things you must do when it comes to your food. That's a little ambiguous, but it will become clearer as you read on. These five things simply have to do with how you prepare or store your foods, as well as things you should consume every day for a successful diet and a healthy body.

1. Cooking your food is not going to harm its electricity.

For a long time, people have been spreading the lie that cooking your food will cause it to lose its electricity. A lot of people live their life thinking, "raw food is better than cooked food." According to Dr. Sebi, food can't be destroyed. You can eat raw, you can eat it cooked, you can grind it into carbon and drink it, but it is still going to be electrical. If what you are eating is real food, you are not going to be able to destroy its energy.

You can't destroy any other energy, so why would you be able to destroy the energy in food? You can change its state, but you cannot destroy its energy. There are things that people call food, but it's not real food. It is basically just garbage because it is full of starch. In an interview, Dr. Sebi talked about people who eat "raw foods" because it is "healthier." He said that when he first arrived in New York, there were many "raw" people, but they were eating raw starch, and they were anemic. They may have been eating "raw food," but it wasn't real natural food.

You can eat food in any state that you want to because it cannot be destroyed. Food is energy, and energy cannot be destroyed. Just like Dr. Sebi has repeated time and time, why would his diet have been able to cure people of leukemia and AIDS if cooked foods lost their electricity?

2. Consume plenty of alkalizing beverages every day, and it doesn't have to be just water.

You are supposed to drink a gallon of spring water every day, but you don't have to confine yourself to just plain spring water. You can get its alkalizing effects along with the benefits of other foods by mixing them into a delicious alkalizing beverage. One of the best things you can do for your body is to start every day with a glass of warm lime water.

As we all know, the body is made up of 60% water. Water helps to flush toxins out of the body, keeps you energized, and prevents dehydration. When you add lime, you are adding antioxidants. Limes are full of magnesium, calcium, vitamins A, B, C, and D, and potassium. Drinking lime water can help to promote healthier and younger-looking skin. The antioxidants found in the lime helps to strengthen collagen, and the water will hydrate the skin. Lime water will also help your digestion. Limes work with your saliva to break down your food so that your stomach doesn't have as much work to do. This can help prevent constipation and acid reflux. Its vitamin C content can also help your out during the cold and flu season. The citric acid present in limes can also help to boost your metabolism, which will help you to store less fat and burn more calories.

Lime water isn't the only option you have. You can also enjoy any tea made from the approved herbs list. One of the most popular choices is ginger tea. Ginger is high in magnesium, vitamin C, and other minerals. Ginger tea can help to relieve nausea. It is a favorite among people who tend to suffer from motion sickness when traveling. A cup of ginger tea before you travel can help to prevent vomiting and nausea. If you are sick, drinking a cup of ginger tea at the first signs of nausea will help keep it at bay. Ginger tea is also able to help relieve congestion associated with a cold and allergies. Ginger tea is also able to improve your digestion. Drinking a cup of tea after you eat can help prevent bloating. It is also a great drink for people who have arthritis or other joint problems. Ginger tea can also help to relieve stress.

3. Keep your food storage and prep healthy to keep your food healthy.

Remember all of the Tupperware your mother collected over the years. Think about holiday gatherings with food wrapped in plastic wrap and those Styrofoam take-home containers from your favorite restaurant. While those may be convenient and affordable, they aren't conducive to a healthy lifestyle. Plastic has invaded our life in every way possible only because it is cheap, but what it does to our health and our environment is a high price to pay in the long run. Most Americans only recycle 14% of their plastic packaging, so most of this stuff ends up on our streets or landfills.

Anything your food touches have a chance to leech into your food, but this happens with plastic at a much higher rate than others. There are lots of different types of plastics, and substances get added to plastics to change how flexible it is, stabilize it, and shape it. BPA is one substance that gets added to plastic to make polycarbonate plastics. Phthalates are another substance that gets added to plastics to make them flexible and soft. Polycarbonate plastics are used in food storage containers, plastic plates, reusable water bottles, and even in the receipt you get at the store. Metal cans also contain BPA-based liners so that the foods inside aren't able to corrode the can. Paper cups are lined with BPA as well so that your coffee doesn't leak through as quickly. Most plastic containers will have a code on the bottom. If you see a number from 3 to 7, it could have BPA.

Phthalates are found in many different products and can be harder to know if they are in certain items. They are in cosmetics, water, plastics, food, drugs, dust, and the air. Since 2008, manufacturers have removed some forms of phthalates from children's toys, and there are some countries that have banned them in packaging. The best way to avoid phthalates is to look for PVC or number 3. The Fair Packaging and Labeling Act require manufacturers to mark phthalates, but it is not required when they are used in fragrance.

While the FDA considered BPA to be safe and that all plastics are tested and are supposed to be stable, it still has an effect on your health. Research has found that phthalates and BPA can mimic hormones, which can create an endocrine disruption. The endocrine system affects things from our sleep and immunity to our reproduction and growth. Even BPA-free containers aren't free from problems.

To make sure that your food stays healthy and doesn't soak up any of those bad chemicals present in plastic, it is important that you choose storage containers and prep items that are not made from plastic. Glass containers should be your best friend. Mason jars are a great option because they come in many different sizes, are inexpensive, and are reused. You drink out of them, store salads, and soups, as well as seeds, nuts, spices, and herbs. Mason jars can also be used as lunch containers not to have to use plastic baggies.

There are also other glass storage containers out there if you don't want to store everything in mason jars. You can even find some that are made from tempered glass so that they aren't easily broken.

Stainless steel is also a good option. There are many different sizes and shapes, and you can find them in bento box-styles, insulates, and leak-proof. They tend to be more durable than glass containers, which is good if you have children. The important thing is to make sure that you buy 100% food-grade stainless steel and not aluminum. You will also want to make sure that your cutting board is not made from plastic as well.

4. You should make your veggie stocks and nut milk.

While everybody loves buying pre-made stocks and milk because of convenience, they may not be the best option for your health. When you purchase something pre-made, you have no idea what is in them. If you make them on your own, you will know what you are putting in them. When it comes to vegetable stock, the store-bought kind has a lot of salt in it, and it probably isn't pure sea salt. They probably used vegetables that aren't on the approved list as well. The great news is, making your vegetable stock isn't that hard. All you need is spring water, approve vegetables and some spices. Allow them to boil together for some time, and you have vegetable stock. You'll also find that it tastes a lot better than the store-bought kind.

As far as nut milk goes, it's pretty hard to find one that fits on the approved list. Almond and cashew are the most common. Get this; almond milk doesn't even contain real almonds. One industry insider has stated that a half-gallon of almond milk has less than a handful of almonds. Most of them also contain additives. A lot of vegan milk products contain carrageenan, which comes from seaweed and acts as a thickener. There is a lot of interest concerning carrageenan. Some say it is a carcinogen and others say that it can cause inflammation, ulceration, and contains no nutritional benefits. If you like using nut milk, and there are Dr. Sebi recipes that call for walnut milk, you will need to make your won. Making your own nut milk isn't that hard to do, either.

5. Buy your produce at the farmers market when you can.

Shopping at a local farmers market gives you access to locally grown and fresh foods. The foods there are at the peak of the season, so they will be fresher and taste better. The produce has traveled thousands of miles to get to you, either. It probably doesn't contain any wax coatings or sprays, either. You are also face-to-face with the farmer, which gives you a chance to ask them about the product and find out how it was grown. You may also find produce at the farmers market that isn't available at your local grocery store, and the prices might be a little more reasonable.

Before You Begin

There are many different types of cleanses, from fasting to whole foods, but they all aim to accomplish the same thing, and that is to get rid of inflammatory substances and toxicity. Then they provide your body with pure forms of nutrients. The goal of a cleanse is to heal and restore your body to its optimal health and give its powerful detoxification systems to work without the blockages that are normally there.

The occasional detox is great for the body, but you should never just jump straight into a detox. Getting your body ready for the detox is just as important as the actual detox. If you already follow a very healthy and clean diet, then you won't have as much to do to get ready. But if you are like most people and follow a standard American diet, then you will have some work to do.

Cleanse and detox are words that tend to be used interchangeably, but they aren't quite the same thing. A cleanse is something that you do that will cause detoxification. Your body detoxes naturally as soon as your food has been digesting. This is where it will remove toxic and foreign materials.

Unfortunately, the regular lifestyle and diets of most people causes them to accumulate more toxins than the body is able to purge. Because of this, we need to, on occasion, do a cleanse or fast where we consciously reduce the number of toxins that we are consuming so that the body is forced into a natural detoxifying state.

A cleanse could be a complete abstinence from food or toxic activities, and you only consume water. This type of fast might be helpful, but it's pretty hard to keep up. The Dr. Sebi detox won't require you to stop eating altogether, but if you want to try that type of cleanse, feel free to because it can do amazing things to your body.

Starting just a few days before you plan on beginning your detox, you will want to start changing how you eat. You will need to eat simple, light foods like salads, soups, or veggies. You will want to focus on raw veggies and leafy greens. This is especially true if you haven't been much of a clean eater. You need to give your body a chance to get ready for the cleanse. Take little steps by slowly cutting out processed and sugar foods, and star to increase your intake of fresh foods and grains.

Taking these small steps will increase your body's alkalinity to help it get ready for the deeper cleanse of your detox. During the detox, your body is going to end up releasing toxins that are stored in your tissues. These toxins may enter your bloodstream and can end up causing trouble sleeping, mood swings, body odour, bad breath, aches and pains, or rashes. By preparing for your detox, you can minimize your chances of developing these side effects.

To help you out, we will go over some tips on getting your body ready for your detox.

Dietary Changes

- Begin Your Day Right

You should start adding in a glass of warm lime water to your daily routine. This helps to jump-start your digestion and boost your metabolism. Lime juice is very alkalizing to your body, rich in vitamin C, and helps to cleanse your liver, which are all very important parts of detoxification.

- Switch Up Your Drinks

You will want to start drinking more spring water during the day, and start adding in some cleansing herbal teas, such as burdock, dandelion root, or nettle tea. This is also the best time to switch from regular tap water to spring water. You have to drink spring water while on Dr. Sebi's detox.

If you drink alcohol or coffee, you need to start cutting back on your consumption of them. You won't be able to have them on the detox. To let go of coffee, a good alternative is herbal or green tea. While green tea does contain caffeine, it is full of antioxidants, which will help your detoxification. Sodas and energy drinks should also be eliminated.

Water will play a very big part in your life, so beginning your day with two glasses of water is helpful in getting ready for your detox. If you choose to do the hot lime water that counts towards a glass.

- Keep Things Simple

Start to change your meals to something that is very simple and easy to make. You should opt for dishes that are heavy in natural fruits and vegetables and start weaning yourself off of meats, if you are a meat eater. Include a lot of foods that are rich in chlorophyll because these aid in detoxification.

This can also include drinking veggie soups and broths. If you find it hard to eat enough vegetables, you can get your veggie intake through smoothies or juice. An easy way to add more fruits and veggies into your current diet is by adding a piece of organic fresh fruit to your breakfast each morning. You can also turn to fresh fruits as your mid-afternoon snack instead of heading to the vending machine. When picking out your fruits and veggies, go with organic, seasonal, and local produce when you can so that you avoid pesticides.

- Reduce Your Animal Product Intake

You are going to have to cut out animal products completely on Dr. Sebi's fast, so leading up to it, you should start weaning yourself off of them. The first place to start is to stop eating processed and red meats. This includes things like cured meats and sausages. Choosing leaner meats and fish is a better choice during this time. When picking fish, stay away from fish that are high in mercury, like mackerel and tuna. Fish like salmon, scallops, anchovies, and shrimp are better options.

- Check Your Oils

A lot of people will cook with vegetable or canola oil because the health industry tells you they are better because they are lower in fat, but they aren't. You need to start using olive oil, avocado oil, coconut oil, and grape seed oil. Coconut and olive oils should not be cooked and should only be used raw. You can also use these oils along with some lime juice and herbs to create your own salad dressings.

- Up Your Grain Intake

Right now, you don't have to worry about eating Dr. Sebi approved grains. All you need to worry about is increasing how much whole grains you eat. Start eating more brown rice or spelt, and also start eating more pseudo-grains like quinoa. You need to start reducing how much refined foods like pasta and bread you consume, and that includes whole-grain bread or pasta. Do your best to avoid wheat wherever you are able to.

- Get Rid of Refined Sugar

You have to start reading nutrition levels to make sure that foods aren't hiding sugars. Before the detox, you can pick healthier sugar alternatives in moderation. Maple syrup, raw honey, rapider sugar, coconut blossom syrup, coconut sugar, or agave nectar are great alternatives. Once the detox starts, you will only be able to have agave nectar.

- Get Rid of Table Salt

Table salt does not provide you with any nutrients. Your body also has a very hard time metabolizing table salt. While you are checking nutrition labels for sugars, check and make sure they aren't hiding any table salts. The majority of processed foods will have large amounts of chemically processed salts. You should use sea salt as your salt source. It is full of minerals and they are able to help get rid of heavy metals within your body.

- Cut Out Unhealthy Foods

Leading up to the detox, you should slowly start cutting out unhealthy foods that you like to eat. This includes things like store-bought cookies or muffins, chips, and fried foods. Choose, instead, to snack on homemade dried fruit, seeds, and unsalted nuts. Before the detox, feel free to try some raw chocolate to help you with your chocolate fix.

Chapter 6: Classification Of Foods

Foods are classified into different forms depending on whether they contain acids, and alkaline. Examples of foods are hybridized food, raw foods, live food, Genetically Modified Foods (GMO), Drugs, and dead foods.

Hybridized Foods

They are foods that are not natural. They are created and formed by cross-pollination. The vitamins and mineral levels cannot be quantified and they cannot be grown naturally.

Foods that are cross-pollinated (hybridized) lack proper mineral balance that is present in wild foods. Consumption of hybridized foods results in a lack (deficiency) of minerals in the body.

Fruits and vegetables that are hybridized result in excessive stimulation of the body which subsequently results in loss of minerals in the body.

It is reported that hybridized foods lack electrically charged components. This is because most soils in the world especially the United States lack minerals thereby affecting the foods that are planted on them. In as much as the soil lack minerals, the crops planted on them will automatically lack minerals.

This implies that most foods we eat daily are junk. Junks foods are reported to be void of nutrition and this results in several health problems.

Hybrid foods are mostly sugars that cannot be identified by the body's digestive system. Examples are cows, pigs, watermelon, chicken, sausage roll…and many others.

The Engineers that are involved in producing hybridized foods always conclude that they are doing it for individual to get enough food for consumption but unknowingly, they are causing us more harm than good.

Raw Foods

Raw foods are living foods that have not undergone processing and they are undercooked. They are foods that are dried with the use of direct sunlight and are majorly organic foods.

When raw foods are eaten, there is a high tendency that the individual loses weight because it helps the digestive system to quickly digest the foods. This implies that raw foods are beneficial for those who have the intension of losing weight and are ready to keep lean and clean.

These foods also contain many components needed for the digestion process and are destroyed within a short time if not properly dried.

Raw foods help in the improvement of overall health and can help in fighting against disease-causing organisms. Many individuals that inculcate the habit of eating raw food spend little or zero monies in the hospital because their immune system is competent.

However, other dieters believe that raw foods could contain poison that might cause harm to the body. They, therefore, advise that raw foods should be cooked to remove some toxic substances in it. Such foods include undercooked meat, chicken, fish...and more. They concluded that cooking food helps in killing every viable bacterial and other disease-causing organisms that may be present in them.

Live Foods

Live foods are foods that are not dead without consuming them. All live foods do not contain toxic components when they are left to undergo fermentation.

They are foods that are not processed, cooked, microwaved, irradiated, genetically modified, drenched with chemicals (pesticides, insecticides, and preservatives).

Moreso, living foods do not undergo destruction when they are not in their environment. The materials required for the process of digestion are embedded in the living food which contains almost the same pH with water.

Therefore, live foods help the body to become re-energized and cause it to be in the state that is fit to fight any disease. it is also important in detoxifying the body in the intercellular and intracellular level.

Genetically Modified Foods (GMO)

These are food improved by a man with the use of genetics. They mostly damage the immunity in the body. These foods form an abnormal approach in humans and also cause genetic consequence in the body.

Genetically modified foods contain genes of allergen which facilitates allergic reactions in the body. Excess consumption of Genetically Modified Foods is reported to be associated with the inability to resist bacteria in the body.

Examples are foods that are grown hastily, weather-resistant foods such as corn, yeast, brown rice...and many others.

Drugs

Many drugs are dangerous and harmful to the body. They are extremely toxic and acidic. Most of them are extracted and are synthetic.

Drugs can influence and affect several body organs thereby reducing the immune system, increasing the susceptibility of infections and diseases, as well as causing cardiovascular problems.

Examples are cocaine, sugar, all prescription drugs, heroin…and many others.

Dead Foods

These are foods that when fermented become toxic and they have a prolonged life span. They are overdone and over-processed foods.

Dead foods are associated with the risk of having depression, cancer, untimely death, cardiovascular diseases and problems, poor digestion as well as diabetes.

Dead foods facilitate the accumulation of fatty tissues in the body which could result in the above-listed health problems.

Dead food is void of nutrients because the refining process has taken almost all the nutrients (fibers, vitamins, minerals) available in it.

Most of the dead foods are very tasty and inviting in that you continue eating them without stopping. As a result, you become fat and feel sick.

Examples are deep-fried foods, synthetic foods, white rice, sugar, soft drinks, snacks, desserts, alcohols, sugars…and many more.

The Importance of Dr. Sebi Nutritional Diets

All Dr. Sebi's recommended diets are majorly live foods that add benefits to the body and also improve the overall health. Hence, the benefits are:

- o It helps in the prevention and treatment of cancer.
- o It helps in the prevention and treatment of stroke.
- o It helps in the prevention and treatment of high blood pressure.
- o Cholesterol is absent in his diets.
- o Alcohol is absent in his diets.
- o It contains very low saturated fats which also prevent major heart-related diseases.
- o It helps in the prevention and treatment of Diabetes.
- o It helps in weight loss.

- o It contains very low fat which prevents heart diseases and other heart malfunctions.

- o It contains no processed sugar.

- o It helps in controlling your appetite.

- o It helps in the reduction of susceptibility to diseases.

Chapter 7: Best Alkaline Foods

Almost all of the alkaline forming foods could be considered as being superfoods. It isn't just because of their ability to help the body keep a healthy pH balance but because of the nutrient density. Alkaline forming foods are plant based and have many healing properties.

You might know that it is very healthy to drink warm lime water or fresh green juice. They can improve the body's ability to detox, boost the immune system, and give you a huge dose of nutrients. This is because all of these can help raise the body's pH level and this turns your system from being acid to alkaline.

If you were a good student during chemistry class, you might remember the concept of alkali and acid. If you don't, then here is a refresher course. Acids will have a pH level less than seven where alkalis will have a pH level or greater than seven. Water is the most neutral with a pH of seven. Basically, this means that acids will be corrosive in nature and sour in taste. Alkalis will be used to neutralize acids.

When the body is in an alkaline state, it will become more disease resistant that inhibits the growth of organisms such as cancer, fungi, yeast, viruses, and bad bacteria. The oxygen levels get raised in our blood, organs, and tissues. This enable them to function more efficiently and effectively. It can reduce the acidity and helps keep the alkaline state that helps encourage toxin excretion, energy production, and healthy cell turnover.

There are several factors that can impact our body's pH levels. The easiest way is by what we eat. When we eat alkaline forming foods and minimize how much acid forming foods we eat, our bodies can keep up the alkaline state. Any alkaline forming food will be plant based and are rich in antioxidants, minerals, and vitamins. These are easier to digest, and this improves the gut's immune function and helps lower mucus production and inflammation.

While our bodies are digesting our foods, the stomach secretes gastric acid. This helps to break down the food. Our stomachs will have a pH of between 2.0 and 3.5. This is very acidic, but we need it to be able to digest our foods right. But there are times when because of bad food habits or bad lifestyle choices, the acid level gets haywire and this can cause gastric ailments, acid reflux, and other problems. If you were to look at the normal diet of any American, it will contain huge amounts of acidic foods like pastries, doughnuts, colas, kebabs, bacon, sausages, cheese sandwiches, rolls, pizza, samosa, burgers, and many more that could cause the acidic balance in our stomachs. When these foods get broken down, it leaves behind a residue that is called acid ash. This is the chief cause of stomach problems. Foods that are acidic in nature once they are digested by our body are processed foods, refined sugars, whole grains, eggs, dairy products, and meats. You need to know that a food's alkaline or acid tendency doesn't have anything to do with the pH of the food itself. Limes are acidic in nature but does have an alkalizing effect on our bodies. Alkaline foods are needed to bring our bodies in balance. Like many doctors and experts have said for years, we have to have a meal that is balanced with everything instead of restricting ourselves to just eating one category of food. Alkaline foods can help counter the risks of acid reflux and acidity and this will bring us some relief.

Alkaline Foods You Should Eat

Alkalizing foods aren't what you think. It turns out that there are some pretty good options out there.

Here is a list of the best alkalizing foods that are versatile and delicious. Any of these can be used alongside any other alkalizing vegetable or fruit to help cleanse the body from toxins that are slowly killing us.

- Kale

There is a very good reason that kale has been called the new beef. It is high in vitamin K, calcium, and plant iron. These can help protect you against some cancers. Kale is one of the most alkaline foods out there.

Kale is mild in flavor and can kick up any recipe. You can add kale to any smoothie that calls for greens. Add it to soups, salads, and stir fries for a wonderful alkaline boost.

- Cherries

Cherries are a great source of antioxidants like anthocyanins that can prevent cancer. Studies have shown that cherries can help inflammation associated with arthritis and joint pain. They could even help prevent cardiovascular disease.

Cherries can be put into any smoothie. They are great in a post workout shake because they contain protein and alkalizing nutrients.

Any post-workout smoothie needs to include alkaline foods because lactic acid gets released when you exercise. Lactic acid helps increase energy. Lactic acid makes the body more acidic; this is why it is important to get rid of the acidity by eating more alkaline foods after you exercise.

- Pears

These wonderful fruits are low in sugar but high in fiber. This makes them a wonderful fruit for anyone who has blood sugar problems. They are high in vitamin C which in turn helps protect cells from carcinogens.

- Zucchini

This is a great source of phytonutrients like lutein. Lutien is in the same antioxidant family as beta carotene, this means it has better benefits for protecting your eyesight.

Zucchini is now a very popular vegan, gluten free, low carb pasta alternative. Zucchini noodles are easy to make by using a spiralizer that you can find pretty much anywhere.

It is easy to throw together a quick zucchini pasta but pairing it with basil, other spices, and vegetables.

- Strawberries

This is another fruit that is a great source of vitamin C. They also have manganese. Manganese is a trace mineral that help the body's metabolic function.

You can enjoy strawberries in a variety of ways. They can add the smallest amount of sweet to any dish. They are for using in smoothies. Just freeze them and you won't have to use ice.

- Apples

Apples have always been considered to be the healthiest food around. This is because they are full of antioxidant like vitamin C, detoxifying fiber, and flavonoids that can protect you against cancer. These nutrients are great for helping with cholesterol and high blood pressure.

To get more benefits from your apples, try adding them to dishes you normally wouldn't consider putting them into.

- Watermelon

Watermelons give our bodies essential electrolytes for heart health like potassium. Because watermelons are made up of mostly water, it can help keep you hydrated better than other vegetables and fruits.

Watermelon is a great snack by itself, but it is fun to be creative. Make a smoothie out of watermelon, ginger, agave syrup, and a dash of cayenne.

- Other Leafy Greens (Dandelion, Amaranth, Turnip, Sea Vegetables)

Almost all leafy greens will have an alkalizing effect on our bodies. It isn't any wonder that our ancestors and doctors always tell us to eat out greens. The have essential minerals that are needed for our bodies to carry out their functions. You can add sea vegetables, turnip greens, amaranth greens, and dandelion greens to any smoothie or meal.

- Key Limes

Most people think that since limes are highly acidic, they would have an acidic effect on our bodies, but they are actually they are a great alkaline food. Limes are also loaded with vitamin C and can help detoxify our bodies while giving relief from heart burn and acidity.

- Sea Salt and Seaweed

Sea salt and seaweed have about 12 times more minerals that greens that are grown in the ground. They are a very alkaline food and can give your body many benefits. You can add in some kelp or nori to your stir fry or soup. Using sea salt as your main seasoning can bring more alkalinity to your body.

- Walnuts

Many people love to munch on walnuts when they feel hunger kicking in. Other than being a great source of healthy fats, they create an alkalizing effect in our bodies. Because they are high in calories, you need to limit the amount you eat.

- Onion

Onions including red onions are the most important ingredient in Indian cooking and they bring lots of flavor to your dishes. If you cook them in a healthy oil like avocado oil, it will increase their alkalinity. Eating them raw is a great choice since onions have many nutritional benefits other than being alkaline forming. They have anti-bacterial and anti-inflammatory effects and are full of vitamin C. You can use them in many different ways to spice up your tea, soup, or stir fry.

- Tomatoes

These will be at their most alkalizing when they are eaten raw. They do contain many nutrients whether raw or cooked. They are full of vitamin C, vitamin B6, and digestive enzymes. Vitamin B6 is very difficult to find naturally. Eat a slice tomato as a snack with a sprinkle of sea salt or add it to your favorite omelet or salad.

- Avocado

This is a powerhouse of deliciousness and nutrients. Avocados contain lots of healthy fats plus they are heart healthy, anti-inflammatory, and very alkalizing.

- Basil

Basil is the tastiest alkalizing ingredient. It is high in calcium, vitamin K, and vitamin A. It is high in flavonoids that have antioxidant effects.

- Mushrooms

Mushrooms contain antioxidants, minerals, vitamins, and protein. They can have many benefits to our health. Antioxidants are chemicals that can help keep our bodies get rid of free radicals.

Free radicals are byproducts of bodily processes and metabolism. They get trapped in our bodies and if too many are trapped, oxidative stress could happen. This could harm the body's cells and could lead to many health problems.

Mushrooms contain choline, vitamin C, and selenium. The antioxidants in mushrooms could help prevent breast, prostate, lung, among other kinds of cancers. Mushrooms can also help with heart health, diabetes, and during pregnancy. Mushrooms are high in B vitamins like niacin, pantothenic acid, thiamine, folate, and riboflavin. These help the body form red blood cells and get energy from food.

Conclusion

Dr. Sebi's diet is based on a list of pre-approved nuts, seeds, oils, herbs, vegetables, fruits and cereals. As animal products are not allowed, the diet is well thought-out as a vegan diet. He proposed that for your body to heal itself, you must have and monitor the diet constantly for the rest of your life. Dr. Sebi's diet promotes the consumption of whole, unprocessed and herbal foods. This can help you lose weight if you recently adopted this healthy eating lifestyle. However, this largely depends on how often you take these diets and how committed you are to it. It is somehow restrictive but will be of great benefit at the end turns your body into an alkaline state. There are both benefits and downsides to following any diet regime. The Alkaline diet holds both of these. We believe that the positives outweigh the negatives, and in fact, understanding the negatives may indeed lead to further positives. It is the application of an alkaline diet in practice, and an increased mindful focus on what we put into our bodies, that provides the greatest benefit. This is what we hope the sum takeaway is from our guide, and from the late Dr. Sebi's teachings.

This journey may be difficult and challenging to begin. It is a fundamentally different way of eating and thinking about eating that runs contrary to the modern American diet and mythology of food production. Mental preparation will be your ally, and a dedication to yourself is required. This is more of a lifestyle than a fitness diet, so be prepared for substantial change. However, on the other side of this journey lies a healthier, happier you.

It is not recommended to partake in this diet as a means to try and treat an ailment or to lose weight. An alkaline diet is solely designed to reduce acidity. Additional benefits may arise, but these are helpful byproducts of an alkaline-focused system. Always consult with a medical practitioner if you have a pre-existing condition, or are within a risk group, including those who are pregnant or elderly. For best results, follow the recommended alkaline diet as closely as you can. Provide your body with the most nutrients possible to help it recover from a lifetime of acidity. Incorporating certain elements of the diet is a great first step, but do your best to explore how far you can take your diet. Check your local grocers for their produce variety, and reach out to specialty stores for herbs and unique vegetables. Dr. Sebi's methods of cleansing the body in a natural, organic way still inspire many herbalists today. His initial discoveries are used as a base in many other alkaline meal plans that you will discover. Focus on your body, focus on your mind, and focus on you. Having achieved the guidelines for a healthy and fit life with the help of the alkaline diet book, I will gladly say that Dr. Sebi alkaline diet is a very effective weight loss diet and effective for quick results. Thank you for reading. Enjoy a healthy life.

CPSIA information can be obtained
at www.ICGtesting.com
Printed in the USA
BVHW061627180521
607636BV00008B/800